'One of the most urgent needs of the church is the re-articulation of ancient and fundamental doctrines, in a style that is both accessible and winsome. That is what Melvin Tinker offers for the incarnation, borrowing the title from the Christmas carol with the lines 'Veil'd in flesh, the Godhead see; / Hail th'incarnate deity!' Unpacking parts of Hebrews 1, and then reflecting on an array of topics tied to the incarnation, Tinker brings his readers along with easy prose, eager to show how this essential Christian truth works out in the lives of Christians. This book could be usefully read by folk who are not yet Christian believers but who would like to gain a better grasp of what Christians think, and by Christians who are still a little wobbly about the non-negotiable tenets of the faith.'
D. A. Carson, Research Professor of New Testament, Trinity Evangelical Divinity School, Deerfield, Illinois, USA

'There is no subject more important for Christians than the person and work of Jesus and so there is no subject more profitable for us to explore. Melvin Tinker has given us a great starting point, combining biblical insight with theological reflection while always keeping practical application in view. Prepare to be stretched, but in this case being stretched will make your life deeper rather than thinner.'
Tim Chester, faculty member of Crosslands Training and pastor of Grace Church, Boroughbridge

'In his latest book, Melvin Tinker takes pains not to compromise the great mystery of the incarnation, that God was in Christ reconciling the world unto himself. He writes insightfully, with new modes of expression, and dips into a great store of examples. He's familiar with the great Christian minds who have stretched their thinking about the very apex of our faith. He follows them in ways that respect the 'mystery of godliness', and encourages the reader to think along with them. Doctrine may divide, but it's certainly not dull, dry or dead. Not, at least, while Melvin's around.'

Paul Helm, formerly Professor of the History and Philosophy of Religion, King's College, London

'The incarnation is such an overwhelming doctrine – so central in its immediacy, so vast in its implications, so deep in its importance – that we can almost excuse preachers and teachers who feel too intimidated to dwell on it in much detail. But there is a way to ponder the depths of this doctrine without falling into error or drifting into unprofitable speculation. This fine book points out that way: grounded in Scripture, guided by the great creeds and confessions, nourished by spiritual experience and always within easy distance of pastoral application, *Veiled in Flesh* is an invitation to deep reflection on the incarnation.'

Fred Sanders, Professor of Theology, Torrey Honors Institute at Biola University

'This is a thoughtful and informed exploration of the profound truth that is at the centre of Christian faith: that through Christ we are encountered by God in all of his greatness and goodness. This is the message we hear from Scripture and this is what shines its bright light into our dark world. I commend this excellent study.'

David F. Wells, Distinguished Research Professor, Gordon-Conwell Theological Seminary

VEILED IN FLESH

VEILED IN FLESH

The incarnation – what it means
and why it matters

Melvin Tinker

INTER-VARSITY PRESS
36 Causton Street, London SW1P 4ST, England
Email: ivp@ivpbooks.com
Website: www.ivpbooks.com

First published 2019

British Library Cataloguing-in-Publication Data
A catalogue record for this book is available from the British Library.

ISBN: 978-1-78974-096-7
eBook ISBN: 978-1-78974-097-4

Set in Minion Pro
Typeset in Great Britain by CRB Associates, Potterhanworth, Lincolnshire
Printed and bound in Great Britain by Ashford Colour Press Ltd, Gosport, Hampshire

Inter-Varsity Press publishes Christian books that are true to the Bible and that communicate the gospel, develop discipleship and strengthen the church for its mission in the world.

IVP originated within the Inter-Varsity Fellowship, now the Universities and Colleges Christian Fellowship, a student movement connecting Christian Unions in universities and colleges throughout Great Britain, and a member movement of the International Fellowship of Evangelical Students. Website: www.uccf.org.uk. That historic association is maintained, and all senior IVP staff and committee members subscribe to the UCCF Basis of Faith.

Contents

Part 1
'. . . THE GODHEAD SEE':
A BIBLICAL FOUNDATION

Part 2
'HAIL, THE INCARNATE DEITY':
A THEOLOGICAL EXPLORATION

Foreword

Martin Luther famously emphasized that the doctrine of justification was the main thing. 'If the doctrine of justification is lost,' he declared, 'the whole of Christian doctrine is lost.' Yet there are doctrines even more fundamental. Justification itself rests on Christ's vicarious atonement, and this in turn rests on the doctrine of the incarnation. The man on the cross, dying in grief and agony for our sins, was 'the Lord, the King of Glory'.

It is this mystery of the Godhead 'veiled in flesh' that this volume explores, reverently but rigorously, carefully probing the great Christological statements of the New Testament, drawing gratefully on the Church Fathers and the ancient creeds, listening respectfully to the voices of reverent modern theology, and exposing to the light the bizarre speculations of headline-grabbing irreverence. But in case it all sounds too daunting, Melvin Tinker astutely reminds us of C. S. Lewis's observation that making our way through 'a tough bit of theology' is the very best way to make our hearts sing.

But it is not enough for theology to know its own sources and be conversant with its own history. It must also know its audience, and even though it may be speaking (like the New Testament) to those who are already believers, those very believers are influenced, probably far more than they know, by the culture of the world around them. This is no excuse for avoiding tough theology, and there is certainly some tough theology here, especially some serious reflection on what it meant for the divine and the human to be united in one person in Jesus Christ.

We need make no apology for this. Melvin Tinker has every right to assume that every Christian is a theologian, and a keen one, but this doesn't mean that theology has to be heavy going or weighed down with jargon-overload. Plain, straightforward exposition is his aim, and in this he succeeds, presenting tough theology in the accents of the present, and reflecting a mind well conversant with the culture of his age: an age of entrenched scepticism, but still pining over the loss of significance. This is why *Veiled in Flesh* not only plunges us into an extended conversation with the writer to the Hebrews and asks us to listen carefully to the voices of the Church Fathers, but also insists that we hear the sense of loneliness and isolation expressed in modern fiction, movies and drama; and so, while we walk with Gregory of Nyssa and Hilary of Poitiers, we also bump into Woody Allen, Samuel Beckett, the actor Jessica Lange and a converted UVF terrorist, each throwing his or her own unexpected mite into the theological treasury.

But the challenge, to believer and unbeliever alike, is never far away: 'What do you think of Christ?'

Donald Macleod

Preface

Dorothy L. Sayers was a friend and contemporary of C. S. Lewis. Although she is better known for her fictional 'whodunnit' novels (she invented the amateur sleuths Lord Peter Wimsey and Harriet Vane), she had a first-rate theological mind, so much so that the then Archbishop of Canterbury, William Temple, wished to confer upon her an honorary Doctorate of Divinity. In her typical forthright manner she once wrote,

> The Christian faith is the most exciting drama that ever staggered the imagination of man ... the plot pivots on a single character, and the whole action is the answer to a single central problem – What do you think of Christ? The Church's answer is categorical and uncompromising, and it is this: That Jesus Bar-Joseph, the carpenter of Nazareth, was in fact and in truth ... the God by whom all things were made. His body and brain were those of a common man; his personality was the personality of God ... He was not a kind of demon pretending to be human; he was in every respect a genuine living man. He was not merely a man so good as to be 'like God' – he was God.[1]

Since those words were written there have been many who have challenged such a claim.

---

1 Dorothy L. Sayers, 'The Dogma Is the Drama', in *Creed or Chaos?* (New York: Harcourt, Brace and Co., 1949), pp. 20–24.

Preface

When I went up to Oxford to read theology in the early 1980s, a series of essays under the provocative title *The Myth of God Incarnate* had just exploded like a bomb in the theologian's playground. In a nutshell the authors argued that it wasn't possible to formulate the belief that Christ is divine in any intellectually satisfying way. This, however, was of no consequence, the authors argued, since such a belief wasn't central to Christianity anyway, as had traditionally been thought![2] One of the contributors, Dr Don Cupitt, an ordained minister in the Church of England, in a debate on British TV was publicly claimed by the leading atheist A. J. Ayer as 'one of his own'! A damning back-handed compliment if ever there was one.

Just over a decade later, Australian scholar Barbara Thiering, in her *Jesus the Man: A New Interpretation of the Dead Sea Scrolls*,[3] reconsidered the New Testament by reading in between the lines and suggesting, amongst other things, that Jesus was merely a man, was married, produced three children and was divorced, only to marry again.

More recently, the former presiding Bishop of the Episcopal Church in the USA Bishop Katharine Jefferts Schori was asked, 'What does someone do when they believe that Jesus is divine but that some things that are defined as creeds – that Mary was a virgin, for example – don't seem right? Can one still be a faithful Christian?' She replied,

If you begin to explore the literary context of the first century and the couple of hundred years on either side, the way that someone told a story about a great figure was

---

2   John Hick, *The Myth of God Incarnate* (London: SCM, 1979).
3   Barbara Thiering, *Jesus the Man: A New Interpretation of the Dead Sea Scrolls* (London: Corgi, 1993).

to say 'this one was born of the gods'. That is what we're saying. This carpenter from Nazareth or Bethlehem – and there are different stories about where he comes from – shows us what a godly human being looks like, shows us God come among us. We have affirmed ever since then in this tradition that each one of us is the image of God. We are all the sons and daughters of God.[4]

In short, Jesus is only 'god-like' in that he, like the rest of us, bears God's image, and he is an exceptional human only in so far as he 'shows us what God is like' in a way better than any other individual who has yet lived (presumably there is the theoretical possibility that another human being might come along who will be even *more* outstanding and do a better job).

Such views are a far cry from the great Catholic creeds of the church, such as the 'Nicene' Creed which asserts:

We believe in one Lord, Jesus Christ,
the only Son of God,
eternally begotten of the Father,
God from God, Light from Light,
true God from true God,
begotten, not made,
of one Being with the Father.
Through him all things were made.

The present book is an attempt to show that such affirmations of belief are biblically grounded and intellectually coherent.

---

4   '"A Wing and a Prayer": An Interview with Bishop Katharine Jefferts Schori', *Parabola Magazine*, Spring 2007, pp. 12–17, <https://anglicanecumenicalsociety.files.wordpress.com/2010/02/perabola_bishop.pdf>.

In order to make it as accessible to as many people as possible, this book is divided into two parts.

Part 1 (chapters 1 to 5) shows that at the very least one of the early major New Testament writers, the anonymous author of the letter to the Hebrews, in his first chapter lays the foundation for what came to be formulated in the above creed, that, in the words of Sayers, 'Jesus Bar-Joseph, the carpenter of Nazareth, was in fact and in truth . . . the God by whom all things were made.' This is clear, unambiguous and uncompromising.

The approach adopted will involve a plain, straightforward exposition of the text, designed not to satisfy speculation but to fuel devotion. To be sure, this will entail a careful unpacking of some key doctrines regarding the person and work of Christ, but in a way which arises out of the biblical text with a careful eye on pastoral application.

Part 2 (chapters 6 to 11) is a little different. With the help of systematic and historical theology, and especially the way the early church sought to ward off various heresies concerning the second person of the Trinity, we shall delve a little deeper to clarify our own thinking concerning the wonderful mystery of Christmas. We shall ask: 'What is true incarnation? How are we to consider the relationship between the divine nature of Jesus and his human nature in a way which doesn't compromise either? And why is it so important to get our thinking straight?' This is not the stuff of philosophical speculation (although it will involve grappling with some sophisticated ideas) but a humble desire to 'think God's thoughts after him' within the limits of biblical revelation. The approach is that of Anselm, 'faith seeking understanding'.

You might feel daunted by this and so be tempted to stay only with the first part. You are free to do that, of course, but let me encourage you to dig deeper as you are most likely to find this spiritually rewarding in ways which may come as something of a surprise. In his foreword to Athanasius's book on the incarnation (to which we shall be referring), C. S. Lewis wrote,

> I believe that many who find that 'nothing happens' when they sit down, or kneel down, to a book of devotion, would find that the heart sings unbidden while they are working their way through a tough bit of theology with a pipe in their teeth and a pencil in their hand.[5]

You may wish to forego the pipe in following Lewis's example, but the experience he is describing is one many have shared: genuine theological reflection leads to heartfelt devotion, making 'the heart sing'. That has been my experience in writing this book, and hopefully it will be yours in reading it.

Make no mistake, the cardinal belief of the incarnation has transformed the world over the last two thousand years and continues to do so. Any attempt to reduce Jesus to a 'pale Galilean' or some such not only does injustice to the data of the New Testament and the experience of countless men and women throughout the ages and around the world, but it results in a 'pale Christianity' which is no Christianity at all.

I would like to express my deepest appreciation to Mark Lanier and for the use of his splendid library which is second to none, and also for the helpful assistance of the library staff whose 'Southern hospitality' made working in hot, humid Houston a delight. I am also grateful to Philip Tinker for his helpful suggestions which have resulted in this being a better

---

5   *On the Incarnation: St Athanasius, with an Introduction by C. S. Lewis* (Crestwood, NY: St Vladimir's Seminary Press, 1998), p. 8.

book, and to Dr Richard Hawes and Jess Motion for their careful work on the references and the Scripture index.

Finally, as always, I want to thank my wife, Heather, for her tireless support and wise advice.

And so read on and be amazed at 'love so amazing, so divine'. Soli Deo Gloria.

Melvin Tinker
The Lanier Theological Library

Part 1

'. . . THE GODHEAD SEE': A BIBLICAL FOUNDATION

1
God's final word (Heb. 1:1–4)

One of the most popular Christmas carols of all time, written by Charles Wesley and modified by George Whitefield, is 'Hark, the Herald Angels Sing'. It contains the immortal lines: 'Veiled in flesh the Godhead see / Hail, the incarnate deity / Pleased as man with man to dwell, / Jesus, our Emmanuel.' Great words, but what do they actually mean, and do they really matter?

What they mean (as strange and seemingly implausible as it may initially sound) is that the Creator became a creature without ceasing to be Creator. Why they matter is because upon them rest our eternal destiny and the future of the whole universe. This is the way C. S. Lewis summarized the situation in his day, which was not all that dissimilar from ours:

> Is not the popular idea of Christianity simply this: that Jesus was a great moral teacher and that if only we took his advice we might be able to establish a better social order and avoid another war? . . . It is quite true that if we took Christ's advice we should soon be living in a happier world. You need not even go as far as Christ. If we all did what Plato or Aristotle or Confucius told us, we should get on a great deal better. And so what? We never have followed the advice of great teachers. Why are we more likely to start now? . . . But as soon as you look at any real Christian writings, you find that they are talking about something quite different from this popular religion.

They say that Christ is the Son of God ... they say that those who give Him their confidence can also become sons of God ... They say that His death saved us from our sins.[1]

Putting it bluntly, if Jesus is not God who became man, then Christians are guilty of idolatry by worshipping a man, in which case the charge of blasphemy by Muslims is upheld. If Jesus is no more than a man, but simply to be placed on the same level as Socrates or Buddha, we needn't give his words any more weight than those of any other man. But if he is *God*, this is a game changer, for then we can say with a fair degree of certainty that we *know* what God is like, what he wants from us and how we can be related to him.

In the first chapter of the letter to the Hebrews the writer expresses in the most sublime way imaginable that which defies the human imagination and which is meant to lead us into grateful devotion and genuine discipleship: that God became a man without ceasing to be God.

Although we don't know *who* the writer of this letter was, we do know *what* he was, namely, a pastor-preacher. All the evidence is that this is one long sermon,[2] although, according to Hebrews 13:22, it is a rather *brief* sermon! Hebrews 1:1–4 is one long sentence in the original packed with theological dynamite.[3] The author's writing style is not like that of any other writer in

---

1   C. S. Lewis, *Mere Christianity* (Glasgow: Fount, 1978), pp. 133–134.

2   'Hebrews can effectively be described as a carefully argued exposition, employing the midrashic treatment of Scripture repeatedly punctuated by exhortatory passages.' Donald A. Hagner, *Encountering the Book of Hebrews* (Grand Rapids: Baker, 2002), p. 29.

3   While our English versions give a verb for the first clause 'God spoke to our fathers', the Greek actually uses a participle there (we maybe should think of 'speaking' rather than 'spoke'). The real verb doesn't come until the reference to the 'last days' when God spoke by his Son. There we have the main verb of the sentence. I owe this observation to Mark Lanier.

the New Testament – it is highly polished; some would say he is the 'Shakespeare' of the New Testament writers. Harold W. Attridge describes Hebrews as 'a masterpiece of early Christian homiletics, weaving creative scriptural exegesis with effective exhortation'.[4] But it is not so much *how* he writes that is particularly impressive, but *what* he writes.

Let's begin with the first two verses: 'Long ago, at many times and in many ways, God spoke to our fathers by the prophets, but in these last days he has spoken to us by his Son.'

Communication problems

As any marriage counsellor will tell you, most problems in relationships come down to a failure to *communicate*: 'He never listens to me'; 'She doesn't understand me'; 'It's as if we are from different planets: I'm from Mars, she is from Venus, and my mother-in-law is from Pluto!' Effective communication is vital to fostering good relationships between people. If that is the case at the human level, how much *more* so at the divine–human level, between God and people?

This immediately raises some big questions: 'If there is a God, how are we to know? If there is a God, how can we know him?' For both questions to be answered positively, some sort of communication has to take place, and the initiative has to come from God's side. If God is there, then *he* must make himself known, *he* must tell us what he is like, for he is infinite and we are finite, and a great gulf is fixed between us. There is what Søren Kierkegaard called an 'infinite qualitative distinction' between God and us.

---

4 Harold W. Attridge, 'Hebrews', in John Barton and John Muddiman (eds.), *Oxford Bible Commentary* (Oxford: Oxford University Press, 2001), p. 1236.

The word used to describe the activity of God 'making himself known' is 'revelation' (from the Latin *revelatio*), a word which, in the biblical languages, means 'a pulling back of the curtains' so that we can know what or who lies behind them:

> It is knowledge that someone else discloses to us. In Christianity the term is important for it means that God has taken the initiative in disclosing himself to man. That knowledge of God is thought of then not as the end product of diligent human search, but the manifestation of God's grace and of his will to be known.[5]

Here our writer to the Hebrews tells us that God has done just that in very special ways.

In the rather funny film *Love and Death*, the character played by the American comedian Woody Allen at one point says in exasperation,

> If God would only speak to me – just once. If he would only cough. If I could just see a miracle. If I could see a burning bush or the seas part. Or my Uncle Sasha pick up the bill.

What you have in this plea is a mixture of universal human longing and entrenched modern cynicism. People want some assurance there is a God. But then there follow certain conditions: Allen wants God the conversationalist – 'If God would only speak'; but he *has* spoken, maybe not in the way some

---

5   Leon Morris, *I Believe in Revelation* (London: Hodder & Stoughton, 1976), p. 10.

people would want, but he has spoken nonetheless. God has spoken through the cross, but Allen would prefer a cough. Allen wants God the conjurer – 'If I could just see a miracle' – but dismisses a book full of miracles: the Bible. We receive the impression that no matter what conditions are laid down for God to meet, more conditions will be waiting further down the line. In every case it is God who is expected to jump through the hoops of our making and to do so at our bidding.

Not so the real God. However, that is not to say that he is not exceedingly gracious in the way he stoops down to speak to us. He takes into account our frailties and so speaks in ways we can understand, using human language. The French theologian John Calvin speaks of God 'lisping' to us. God also makes allowance for our rebellion, whereby more often than not we don't *want* to understand what he is saying; we are more like Uncle Sasha turning a deaf ear so that someone else picks up the bill at the restaurant!

He is there and he has spoken

Our writer begins with the affirmation that God, having spoken 'in' the prophets in former times, has spoken in these last days 'in' his Son (literal translation). As Jonathan Griffiths rightly concludes,

> Thus his [God's] speech 'in' the Son is personal – even ontological – in its character. Although the terms in which Hebrews expresses this theology of personal reve-lation through the Son differ from the terms of John's prologue, there is here in Hebrews a similar idea: the Son

is himself God's revelatory Word, his speech in personal form.[6]

Here we are told that God has *always* been the speaking God: 'Long ago, at many times and in many ways, God spoke.' Perhaps a better rendering would be 'God *speaking* in the past' is now '*speaking* through his Son' – it is one long continuous event. It is not that God has been silent; it is that sin shrouds our planet in silence and makes us deaf to God and blind to his works. From the very beginning God made us uniquely to know him (Gen. 1 and 2), and since the initial rebellion in Eden he has steadily been unfolding a plan of rescue that would save the world that is lost and bring it back to him. This passage at the very beginning of the book of Hebrews is setting us up for the fact that God *began* the conversation that is Jesus Christ long before the actual incarnation itself.

This is *special* revelation we are talking about – that is, revelation which is given to specific people at specific times with specific content. The Bible makes it plain that the primary way God has chosen to relate to us is the same way in which we relate to each other: by words. Just consider for a moment how the first book in the Bible begins, which establishes the pattern for the way God deals with us in the rest of the Bible: 'In the beginning, God created the heavens and the earth . . . the Spirit of God was hovering over the face of the waters. And God *said*, "Let there be . . .", and there was . . .' (Gen. 1:1–3). The Jewish philosopher Martin Buber tells the story of a rabbi whose reading of the Scriptures never got beyond Genesis 1:3: 'And

---

6 Jonathan I. Griffiths, 'Hebrews and the Trinity', in Brandon D. Crowe and Carl R. Trueman (eds.), *The Essential Trinity: New Testament Foundations and Practical Relevance* (London: Apollos, 2016), pp. 122–138 [123].

God said'; the marvel of a God who speaks and whose word lies at the heart of who he is was too much for him to contemplate. He who is Lord not only lives, he speaks! The expression 'Thus says the LORD' occurs over three thousand times in the Old Testament, a phenomenon which further underscores God's way of communicating. What is more, when God achieved the greatest communication coup ever, bridging the infinite gulf by becoming one of us in Jesus Christ, we are told 'The *Word* became flesh and dwelt among us' (John 1:14). It's all about the Word.

Counter-cultural

It has to be admitted that this goes against the grain of our culture. It is also contrary to much pagan religion. We live in the age of the visual. 'A picture is worth a thousand words' is taken as a truism. 'Seeing is believing' is more than a cliché; it is pretty well basic to the way most people operate. There was only one time in history when the 'sight' and 'sound' of God were united: in Jesus Christ, God's Son, so that as we look at him we see the works and words of God in perfect harmony. But apart from that one moment, the emphasis is undecidedly upon *verbal* communication: God speaking. Even a prophetic vision was always accompanied by verbal interpretation. Think of the difference between seeing and listening and you will begin to understand why God stresses the listening.[7]

First of all, sight is largely intentional whereas hearing is involuntary. Take sight: we open our eyes, but we can shut

---

7   See Os Guinness, 'The Word in the Age of the Image: A Challenge to Evangelicals', in Melvin Tinker (ed.), *The Anglican Evangelical Crisis* (Fearn, Ross-shire: Christian Focus Publications, 1995), pp 156–171.

them. We can turn our heads towards something or turn them away. In short, *we* are the ones in control. Not so with sound: it comes to us and we receive it immediately. We are addressed whether we like it or not. In other words (pun not intended!), the *speaker* is mainly in control, not the listener.

In the second place, sight is mainly to do with *appearance*, whereas words are to do with *meaning*.

You could think of it like this: imagine that you are in a supermarket and you see a man hammering away at the chest of another fellow lying on the floor. What do you do? The man looks like an attacker, so you think of calling the police or at least the shop manager. But then you realize that you should have called the ambulance when the man explains that the person he is leaning over has had heart failure and he is trying to revive him. That is, his *words* give the correct meaning to his *actions*. So it is with God: he gives meaning to life, to why we are here and how we are best meant to live. He speaks, and it is our duty – more than that: our delight – to listen.

Third, Scripture links sight with *sin*, what the apostle John calls 'the lust of the eyes' (1 John 2:16 NIV). Think of Eden. Adam and Eve rejected God's command, his word, but they *saw* the fruit, and it ended in an act of rebellion.

In the fourth instance the Bible associates sight with *idolatry*. In the making of the golden calf in Exodus 32, the irony is that when the people said, 'We will make gods we can *see* to go before us', they took earrings, objects which honour the ear, to make something which honours the eye! This is symbolic of the change from worshipping the true God who speaks, to following false gods they could see but who were dumb.

How does God speak?

A contrast is set up for us in Hebrews 1.

In the *past* God's revelation was *fragmented*, but *now* it is *fully formed*. The writer says that God spoke 'at many times and in many ways'. A better translation would be 'in many *pieces* and in many *ways* God was speaking'. You could say that there had been a drip-feeding of revelation over the previous centuries.

Let me explain.

Through words and actions God had gradually built up a full picture of himself, what he is like and how we are to relate to him. The record of that self-revelation is contained in the first part of the Bible, what we call the Old Testament. I am sure you have seen those jigsaw puzzles of faces in which, when you look more closely, you discover that each piece is a picture in itself. As we turn to the Bible, what we find in the Old Testament is something a little like that: the jigsaw slowly being pieced together with little pictures until eventually we see the face of God in Jesus, the big picture; and as we look at his life and listen to his words, all the little pictures of God in the Old Testament are to be found there too.

'Who' not 'what'

For the Jews the question was never, '*What* is God?' That is the philosopher's question, and usually you get a philosopher's answer: he is 'the Prime Mover', 'the First Cause' or 'the Ground of all Being'! For the Bible, however, the question is, '*Who* is God?'; and three things about the God of Israel stood out from every other religion: namely, that this *one* God was the Creator, Ruler and Redeemer of all things. You find statements peppered throughout the Bible which spell out those truths, like in Isaiah 40 (NIV): 'To whom will you compare me? . . . Lift up your eyes and look to the heavens: who created all these?'– Creator; 'See, the *Sovereign* LORD comes with power' – Ruler; 'Speak tenderly to Jerusalem . . . her sin has been paid for' – Redeemer. All sorts of pictures were given by the prophets like Moses and others in bits and pieces gradually over a period of time, showing us what God is like: that he is a shepherd, a king, a father, a husband; but also God gave people and practices: priests to offer sacrifices because God is righteous, a temple in which to offer them, a king to rule the people, and so on. The fragments of the jigsaw slowly come together until eventually the picture is complete with the coming of Jesus: 'but in these last days he has spoken to us by his Son'. Where do we find out what Jesus is like and what he said? In these very same Scriptures, in the second half which completes the first, that is, the New Testament.

Give me a person, not a proposition

Sometimes you will hear people say, 'I don't worship the Bible, the written Word, I worship Jesus, the living Word. I want to know a person, not a proposition. I don't want an exposition, I want an experience.' However, when you think about it, these are all false options. How can you know Jesus the living Word other than by learning about him in Scripture the written Word? The Jesus of faith *is* the Jesus of history and we have no other access to him but via the Bible. As John Stott rightly observed,

The only authentic Christ is the biblical Christ. What Scripture has done is to capture him, in order to present him to all people at all times in all places. The climax of God's revelation should be described as the historic, incarnate Christ and the total biblical witness to him.[8]

That is what the writer to the Hebrews is claiming. Stott went on to write, 'We should not therefore perpetuate the myth that God's revelation could be personal without being propositional too, deeds without words. We should not share in the modern disenchantment with words. Words matter. Even images need words to explain them.'[9]

Isn't it also the case that the words of a person reflect the *character* of that person? If someone makes promises and keeps them, we know that he or she is reliable. If someone issues warnings of consequences, we know that he or she is moral. If someone offers words of comfort and love, we know that he or she is caring – and so on. That seems to be a fair summary of the God of the Bible.[10]

Transformation, not just information

We must also remember that words aren't just about conveying *information*, getting things across; they are about *action*,

---

8   John Stott, *Evangelical Truth: A Personal Plea for Unity* (Leicester: Inter-Varsity Press, 1999), p. 48.
9   Stott, *Evangelical Truth*, p. 49.
10 '"Let God be proved true" (Rom. 3:4 NRSV). Throughout the Scriptures, God proves himself true by keeping his word. He fulfils his promises; he does what he says. There is thus a covenantal correspondence, a faithful fit, between God's words and God's deeds.' Kevin J. Vanhoozer, 'Augustinian Inerrancy: Literal Meaning, Literal Truth, and Literate Interpretation in the Economy of Biblical Discourse', in J. Merrick, Stephen M. Garret and Stanley N. Gundry (eds.), *Five Views on Biblical Inerrancy*, Counterpoints: Bible and Theology (Grand Rapids: Zondervan, 2013), pp. 199–235 [216].

getting things done. This is vitally important, so let me explain it a little more carefully.

If I say to my wife, 'I love you', I am not just imparting an interesting piece of information about the state of my glands, I am actually *fostering* love, *showing* care, *building* her up, *strengthening* our relationship *through* those words. Not only through words, of course, but words are a vital part of enhancing and enriching the relationship. This is what God does through his book, the Bible, which is why Christians call it 'the Word of *God*'. This is where we hear God's voice clearly, where we discover his will, learn of his ways and get to know his person, as well as receive his tender comfort.

One-time Bishop of Rochester Christopher Chavasse, who was a great influence on a young T. E. Lawrence ('Lawrence of Arabia'), wrote,

> The Bible is the portrait of our Lord Jesus Christ. The Gospels are the Figure itself in the portrait. The Old Testament is the background leading up to the divine figure, pointing towards it and absolutely necessary to its composition as a whole. The Epistles serve as the dress and accoutrements of the Figure, explaining it and describing it. Then while by our Bible reading we study the portrait as a great whole, the miracle happens, the Figure comes to life, and stepping down from the canvas of the written word the everlasting Christ of the Emmaus story becomes himself our Bible teacher, to interpret to us in all Scripture the things concerning himself.[11]

This is true to every Christian's experience.

---

11 Cited in John Stott, *The Bible: Book for Today* (Leicester: Inter-Varsity Press, 1982), p. 34.

When you turn the pages of the Bible and discover Jesus you will find him to be morally beautiful, displaying a wisdom which is enchantingly delightful with a compassion that is captivatingly inspirational. The Bible from beginning to end is fundamentally a book about *God*, and therefore about Jesus who is God (as the writer to the Hebrews is soon going to make crystal clear) – his character and his dealings with us, fallen and failing as we are – so that we can come to know him and increasingly become the people we were created to be and enjoy God as he is meant to be enjoyed.

Does God still speak through this book, enabling people to encounter his Son? Most certainly! Here is a personal account of the former Ulster Volunteer Force (UVF) terrorist David Hamilton:

The police raided my house in the early hours of the morning, and I was arrested. When I went to court I received a total of 44 years. On the day that I was sentenced my mother called into my uncle's house on her way home to tell him the news. My mother was crying and said, 'You know, there's no hope for my son because he is just caught up in this violence. He's just a hopeless case.' There was an old lady sitting there, 83 years of age. She said to my mother, 'That's not true. God can change your son.' My mother just smiled and thanked her. She did not really believe there was much chance of that happening. This lady was able to tell my mother she would pray for me every day that God would change my heart. 14 months later I was sitting in my prison cell. There was a Christian tract on my bed. I remember thinking it was disgusting and I threw it out of the window. I sat on my bed drinking tea and there came a thought at the back of my mind to become a Christian. 'This is terrible. Someone has put dope in my tea. Why am I thinking like this?' I remember looking up at the shelf and seeing the Bible. I thought, 'Even if I wanted to be a Christian, God would say: "Not you, you're too bad, it is only for nice people or good people."' I lifted the Bible down and started to read some verses out of the fly-pages. Then God showed me something I'd never seen before. He showed me he'd kept me alive. The IRA had tried to kill me several times. I thought, 'Why should God not be interested in me if he's kept me alive.' The next day I decided. I said, 'God, I know you're real, but if you are interested in me, take away the violence and the bitterness I have, and change me.' I prayed that prayer on my knees. I asked the Lord Jesus to save me. God changed me that day. I began to read the Word of God and I can honestly say my life changed. After that I led IRA men to the Lord, sex offenders to the Lord and many other men too. God showed me grace in my life.[12]

In these last days God *has* spoken to us by the Son; and he *continues* to speak to us by his Son, as David Hamilton and countless others like him have found for themselves.

But who exactly *is* this Son?

Questions for reflection and discussion

- What barriers exist which make it difficult to know God? How does God speaking in his Son help overcome them?

---

12 *Evangelicals Now*, February 1994.

- How does Jesus complete and fulfil what was said in the Old Testament Scriptures?
- In the light of this chapter, how might you answer the question: 'Who is God?'

Prayer

I confess, Lord, with thanksgiving, that you have made me in your image, so that I can
Remember you, think of you, and love you.
But that image is so worn and blotted out by faults,
So darkened by the smoke of sin, that it cannot do that for which it was made, unless you renew and refashion it.
Lord, I am not trying to make my way to your height,
For my understanding is in no way equal to that,
But I do desire to understand a little of your truth
Which my heart already believes and loves.
I do not seek to understand so that I may believe,
But I believe so that I may understand;
And what is more,
I believe that unless I do believe I shall not understand.
Amen.
(Anselm of Canterbury)

2

God's power and purpose in creation (Heb. 1:2 and 3b)

There are many ways we might describe the twentieth century. It could be spoken of as the Age of Science – the splitting of the atom, the discovery of the DNA molecule, the landing of man on the moon, the development of laser technology, and a thousand and one other amazing achievements.

Others might refer to it as the Century of Broken Dreams. 'Before the Second World War', William Golding wrote, explaining how he conceived his novel *The Lord of the Flies*,

> I believed in the perfectibility of social man ... but after the war I did not because I was unable to. I had discovered what one man could do to another ... I must say that anyone who moved through those years without understanding that man produces evil as a bee produces honey, must have been blind or wrong in the head.[1]

I would describe the twentieth century, and indeed the twenty-first century even more so, as the Age of the Loss of Significance. Whether it is in the plays of Samuel Beckett, the paintings of Francis Bacon or the anguish of films like *The Diary of a Teenage Girl*, you detect a desperate yearning

---

1   William Golding, *The Hot Gates: And Other Occasional Pieces* (New York: Harcourt, Brace & World, 1966), p. 87.

for significance, for having some sense of purpose in life, and yet at each turn savagely being denied it. As far back as 1932, in his famous speech entitled 'My Credo', Albert Einstein opined: 'Our situation on this earth seems strange. Every one of us appears here involuntarily and uninvited for a short stay, without knowing the whys and the where-fore.'[2] The actress Jessica Lange felt the same: 'The main thing that I sensed back in my childhood,' she said, 'was this inescapable yearning that I could never satisfy. Even now at times I experience an inescapable loneliness and isolation.'[3]

However, we shouldn't be all that surprised at this widespread state of affairs amongst those living in the West, given what has been on offer as the two main views regarding the origin of the universe, and so the nature of humankind.

The first is the secularist or humanistic view. This outlook is captured by these words of the atheist philosopher Bertrand Russell, in his *A Free Man's Worship*: 'Man is the product of causes which had no prevision of the end they were achiev-ing; . . . his origin, his growth, his hopes, his fears, his loves and his beliefs, are but the outcome of accidental collocations of atoms.'[4] That is, we come from nowhere and we are going nowhere, and that leaves us precisely . . . nowhere. If we are the result of some cosmic accident then, by definition, we cannot have meaning because accidents have no meaning. In the words of one humanist, H. J. Blackham, 'The most drastic objection to humanism is that it is too bad to be true. The world is one

---

2 Cited in Os Guinness, *Long Journey Home* (Colorado Springs: Water Brook Press; New York: Doubleday, 2001), p. 7.
3 In Guinness, *Long Journey Home*, p. 7.
4 In Guinness, *Long Journey Home*, p. 59.

vast tomb if human lives are ephemeral and human life itself is doomed to ultimate extinction.'[5]

The second view is the Eastern one. Whereas the secularist stresses the material by denying the spiritual, the mystic stresses the spiritual at the expense of the material. What we perceive to be a material world is nothing but illusion: *Maya*. We are attached to the wheel of life, *samsara*, and we need to be released from it somehow, by meditation or reincarnation – maybe having to be reincarnated 35,000 times, some say, until we eventually dissolve into the deathless lake of *nirvana* and become nothing. That's a pretty depressing prospect too.

Whether you look to Western secularism or Eastern mysticism, you find no answer to the quest for significance because according to both accounts there is *no* significance; for one we are a collocation of atoms randomly set in motion; for the other, an extension of some impersonal force in a dream-like existence.

But then we come to two verses in the Bible which act like someone entering a dark, musty building to open the shutters in order to let in the light, and opening the windows to allow fresh cool air to circulate so that we can start to see and breathe again as human beings. These two verses are found in Hebrews 1 verses 2 and 3.

Here we discover why we feel significant in a world which everyone tells us is devoid of significance, because significance isn't something we can *make* ourselves, it is something which is *bestowed* upon us. Only *created* things can have significance and only persons who are created by a personal God can *feel* significant. The only way we are going to have meaning,

---

5   H. J. Blackham, *Objections to Humanism* (rev. edn; Westport, CT: Greenwood Press, 1963), p. 105.

knowing who we are and why we are here, is if the one who made us tells us. This was something the analytical philosopher Ludwig Wittgenstein noted:

> The sense of the world must lie outside the world. In the world everything is as it is or happens as it does happen. In it there is no value – and if there were, it would be of no value. If there is value which is of value, it must lie outside all happening and being-so. For all happening and being-so is accidental. What makes it non-accidental cannot lie in the world, for otherwise this world again would be accidental. It must lie outside the world.[6]

We saw in the previous chapter that God who transcends the world and yet is intimately involved in the world is the one who has actually been doing the telling, for he is a speaking God. According to Hebrews 1:1, in the past God spoke through different people in different ways which are recorded in the Old Testament. Now he *continues* to speak to us finally and clearly through his Son whom we find in the New Testament. It is just *who* this Son is that the writer is going to unpack a little further, and what he has to say is simply stunning and should either leave us in awed silence or move us to adoring praise.

What was 'before' any 'before'?

Let's take a look at the second part of verse 2.

This 'Son', says our writer, is the one through whom God 'created the world' – literally, 'made the ages'. This is just another

---

6 Proposition 6:41 in L. Wittgenstein, *Tractatus Logico-Philosophicus* (trans. Frank P. Ramsey and Charles K. Ogden; New York: Harcourt, Brace & Co., 1922), pp. 31–32.

way of stressing the Son's *eternal existence*. Before the beginning of anything, before any time, before any space, before any epochs (if you can have a 'before' when there is no time or space), there *was* the Son through whom it all came into being.

> Whether or not the doctrine of Christ's pre-existence is true, it is very difficult to believe that it is not taught in these passages. Christ is a Son (without the definite article, Heb. 1:1), not in the same sense as the prophets, but in a sense that sets him apart and alone. Furthermore, he is the One through whom God made the world, not in this case *ton kosmon* but *tous aiōnas* ('the ages', Heb. 1:2); it is difficult to escape the conclusion that the One through whom the successive ages of history were called into being himself existed before these ages.[7]

Let's pause just there.

Our writer is a Jewish Christian who, in all probability, was writing to other Jewish Christians. The one thing the Jews were adamant about and would die for (as some did at Masada in the great rebellion of AD 74) was the belief that there was only *one* God who was the Creator of everything. Here are a few sample verses out of scores of others which spell this out:

> It is I who made the earth
>   and created mankind on it.
> My own hands stretched out the heavens;
>   I marshalled their starry hosts.
> (Isa. 45:12 NIV)

---

7 Donald Macleod, *The Person of Christ*, Contours of Christian Theology (Leicester: Inter-Varsity Press, 1998), p. 53.

You alone are the LORD. You made the heavens, even the highest heavens, and all their starry host, the earth and all that is on it, the seas and all that is in them. You give life to everything, and the multitudes of heaven worship you.
(Neh. 9:6 NIV)

In the words of one Old Testament scholar, 'The [Hebrew Bible] texts show that he is a universal God having power over everything in heaven and earth and that he is the supreme God fulfilling deeds other gods cannot fulfil.'[8]

Hold on to that thought, and as you do so think on this: there was a man who appeared on the public scene at the age of thirty, also a Jew, who most of his adult life had been hanging doors and laying floors in villages north of Jerusalem. He was a builder by trade; more specifically, a carpenter. But before he started doing any of that, as the second person of the Trinity he was doing something else: hanging stars and laying out galaxies, all 200 billion of them! That is the implication of what our writer means when he says 'through whom also he created the world'.

Already in verse 1 the writer has made two categories: prophets through whom God has spoken, and a Son who, in his own person, *is* God speaking. Now he has drawn up a further two categories: created things – atoms, ducks, roses, stars, planets – and the Creator. The Son falls into the *latter* category, the divine category. This Son was able to bring about everything, without, if you will, 'having to think about it'.

---

8 Herbert Niehr, 'The Rise of YHWH in Judahite and Israelite Religion: Methodological and Historical Aspects', in Diana V. Edelman (ed.), *The Triumph of Elohim: From Yahwisms to Judaisms*, Contributions to Biblical Exegesis and Theology 13 (Kampen: Kok Pharos, 1995), pp. 45–74 [67].

If ever my wife is desperate enough to want me to put up some shelves, I have to do some serious thinking. This will involve deciding where the shelves should go, measuring the height and length, deciding which wood to use and how many brackets to buy, and so on. But when God the Son made a universe he 'knew' all things immediately: he is *omniscient*; he didn't have to 'work things out' as we do, from premises to conclusions, because he 'knows' perfectly how things work out the best – every mathematical equation, every source of power, every possibility and non-possibility: he simply knows! Our writer is claiming that the person who was the carpenter was also the Creator!

Your Jesus is too small

Dr Michael Reeves draws attention to how Christians rob themselves at this point in their thinking about Jesus. He says,

> Sadly, so many Christians have a background virus in their understanding of the gospel here. It's not easy to spot. But it eats away at their confidence in Christ. It is this: the sneaking suspicion that while Jesus is a Saviour, he's not really the Creator of all. So they sing of his love on Sunday – and *there* it is true – but walking home through the streets past the people and the places where Real Life goes on, they don't feel it is *Christ's* world. As if the universe is a neutral place. As if Christianity is just something we have smeared on top of Real Life. Jesus is reduced to being little more than a comforting nibble of spiritual chocolate, an imaginary friend who 'saves souls' but not much else.

He concludes, 'The Bible knows of no such piffling and laughable Christlet.'[9]

Straight away this has an implication for us.

If Jesus created you and everything you have, then by definition he owns you – and everyone else, for that matter. You are his by rights. Far from this being an oppressive thing (because no-one likes the thought of being owned by anybody), it is liberating because it means you can find out who you really are and what you were made for, because there is a personal Creator who can tell you. You don't have to keep guessing any more; you can turn to this Jesus and find out. And when you do you will discover that you were made *for* him, to care for his world under his loving guidance – and in doing that you find true significance.

If I were to take hold of an ordinary door key and decide to do with it what I wanted – maybe use it to open a paint can, scrape off some dirt from my shoe or a dozen other things – I am able to do that with the key, but it is an *abuse* of what the key was made for by the person who designed it. A lot of people are doing something like that with their lives. Just as a key is made for a certain lock, so we are made for Jesus. A similar thought is expressed by the apostle Paul in Colossians 1:15–16:

The Son is the image of the invisible God, the firstborn over all creation. For in him all things were created: things in heaven and on earth, visible and invisible, whether thrones or powers or rulers or authorities; *all things have been created through him and for him.*
(NIV)[10]

---

9 Michael Reeves, *Christ Our Life* (Carlisle: Paternoster, 2014), pp. 12–13.
10 All emphasis in Scripture quotations has been added.

Keeping the whole show on the road

According to Hebrews, not only did the Son (whom we now know as Jesus) make the world; he also keeps the world in existence, as we see in the middle of verse 3, 'sustaining *all things* by his powerful word' (NIV).

Let's be clear what this *doesn't* mean.

It doesn't mean that we are to picture the Son straining to hold the universe on his shoulders like some giant Atlas. Rather, the picture is of *moving* things along, just as a child might move a hoop along a road. It's not a static idea, it's dynamic. The dance of countless atoms, the production of every platelet in the blood system, the birth of every baby, the fall of every bird, the generation of supernovas and the direction of all histories – world history, your history and my history – are personally superintended by *God the Son*.

In 1989 newspapers reported the discovery by two Harvard astronomers of a 'Great Wall' of galaxies stretching hundreds of millions of light years across the universe. It is supposedly five hundred million light years long, two hundred million light years wide and fifteen million light years thick (a light year is six trillion miles). It consists of no fewer than fifteen thousand galaxies, each with a million stars, and was described as the 'largest single coherent structure seen so far in nature'.[11]

Hold on to that thought and couple it with this one: as the tiny baby Jesus was gurgling in the animal trough in which his mother laid him for convenience's sake, he, as the eternal Son, was holding that 'Great Wall' in place. The Son (or Word/Logos

---

11 Cited in John Piper, *The Pleasures of God* (Fearn, Ross-shire: Mentor, 2009), p. 93.

as John calls him at the beginning of his Gospel) was directing the course of history, as well as the manufacture of sugar in each leaf on the planet by the remarkable process of photosynthesis. He was also doing all of those things as the eternal Son while he hung nailed to a cross: at no point did he ever cease to be the one who 'upholds the universe by the word of his power', because he has always been and has never ceased to be eternally *God*: it can't be otherwise. Even while a human being, God the Son continued to do God the Son's work – upholding the universe and directing it to its supreme goal. Here is how the sixteenth-century French theologian John Calvin tried to express this mind-blowing thought:

> Even if the Word in his immeasurable essence united with the nature of man into one person, we do not imagine that he was confined therein. Here is something marvellous: the Son of God descended from heaven in such a way that, without leaving heaven, he willed to be borne in the virgin's womb, to go about the earth, and to hang upon the cross; yet he continuously filled the world even as he had done from the beginning.[12]

Even earlier, the Middle Eastern mystic Ephraim the Syrian attempted to plumb the depths of the Word's 'simultaneous presence':

> He was silent as a babe, and yet He was making His creatures execute all His commands . . . The thirty years

---

12 John Calvin, *Institutes of the Christian Religion*, 2 vols. (ed. John T. McNeill; trans. Ford Lewis Battles; Philadelphia: Westminster, 1960), 1:481.

He was in the earth, Who was ordering all creatures, Who was receiving offerings of praise from those above and those below . . . While the Conception of the Son was fashioning in the womb, He Himself was fashioning babes in the womb. Yet not as His body was weak in the womb, was His power weak in the womb! So too not as His body was feeble by the Cross, was His might also feeble by the Cross. For when on the Cross He quickened the dead, His Body quickened them, yea, rather His Will; just as when He was wholly dwelling in the womb, His hidden Will was visiting all![13]

Here, then, is another implication for us.

Imagine that each day when you wake up, all your food is provided for you, all your clothes laid out for you, all you will ever need is simply there. Imagine, if you can, that this keeps happening day after day, month after month, year on year. Someone just comes into your house each night, and the next morning there it all is. Wouldn't you want to find out who your benefactor was? You would naturally think that this must be a very generous person to keep on doing this. At the very least you would want to get to meet him or her in order to express your thanks. According to Hebrews 1:3, the one who gives you breath every single day, who has given you those marvellous children if you have children, who gives you sight so you can see the colour of the trees, and hearing so you can delight in the songs of the birds or a Bach cantata, who gives you the tactile senses so you can feel the softness of a rose petal, and

---

13 *Hymns on the Nativity of Christ in the Flesh* 3, in Philip Schaff, *A Select Library of Nicene and Post-Nicene Fathers of the Christian Church*, Series 2, vol. 13 (New York: Christian Literature Co., 1886–1900), p. 427.

olfactory organs so you can smell its delicate aroma: this person has a name – Jesus. If you don't know him yet, maybe it is about time that you followed that inner yearning so that you can at least express your gratitude to him? And if you do know him, perhaps you should make every effort to get to know him a little bit more, instead of relying on last year's knowledge?

The goal of the universe

Donald A. Hagner helpfully summarizes where we have got to so far:

> In the first five phrases [of Hebrews 1] we encounter statements that require us to identify Jesus with God. The Son is put with God at the beginning and end of time, as instrumental in creation and as the eventual heir of everything at the end of the age. He also functions in a divine capacity throughout all interim time as the one who through an overruling providence makes possible all ongoing existence. These three time frames anticipate what the author will say at the end of his treatise: 'Jesus Christ is the same, yesterday, today and forever.'[14]

Through the Son God made all things and sustains all things, and he is the one *for* whom all things were made, verse 2: 'whom he appointed heir of all things' (NIV). Following his death, resurrection and exaltation – of which the writer

---

14 Donald. A. Hagner, *Encountering the Book of Hebrews* (Grand Rapids: Baker, 2002), p. 43.

will be saying more (e.g. Heb. 2:5–18) – the whole universe which was his by right as Creator is now his by virtue of his being its Redeemer.

Why creation?

Have you ever wondered why God created anything at all? Sometimes we entertain the delusion that maybe God created us because we would be good company for him: lucky God to have creatures like us around; that is bound to cure any bout of divine loneliness!

That can't be right, for at least two reasons.

First, God has never been lonely; he has been completely and totally satisfied within himself, brim-full of joy within his own being as three persons delighting in the love of each other. The Father looks upon the dear face of his Son and he is enraptured, in a way vaguely mirrored by an earthly father looking upon his own child for the first time – but the Father has been doing this for *ever*. Likewise, the Son cannot love his Father enough; he is thrilled by his Father's perfect glory and endless kindness. And the love of the Father and the Son, which is an everlasting fountain of love, is mediated by the third person in the divine 'family', the Holy Spirit. How can a perfect being be in want of *anything*?

There is a second, less positive reason, however, as to why we are not the answer to God's need: far from bringing him joy, we have given him nothing but heartache. The wonderful world in which he has placed us we have ruined. The bodies and minds he has endowed us with we abuse. Even the gift of love is twisted into lust. If ever God is to be thought of as a parent, it must be as a *wounded* parent.

And yet in verse 2 it is said that *everything* is to be thought of as an inheritance, a gift, if you will, for Jesus. The Father so loves his Son that he wants to gift him with a universe! More specifically, he wants to give him a spouse upon whom he can lavish his love into all eternity. Now we are getting a little closer to the answer to why we were made and how we can find lasting significance.

A divine wedding

We tend to think that the world is all about us. It is there for *us* to enjoy; life is for *us* to live to the full, and the more we can do that without anyone telling us what to do, so much the better, for this, we foolishly think, is 'freedom'. The Bible gently disabuses us of that idea and says that this world is all about Jesus, because it was made through him, is kept going by him and is made for him. To be sure, we are involved in this too, but we can only enjoy it as we were designed to enjoy it: namely, if we are properly related to the one who is at the centre of it all – Jesus Christ.

God created a universe in which his Son would be glorified, not so much by being enthroned in regal splendour, but by showing that God at heart is a God of overwhelming grace and love who would die for his bride, the church, so that she might reign in a new universe with her groom by her side. The American theologian Jonathan Edwards expressed this deep truth in the following way:

The creation of the world seems to have been especially for this end, that the eternal Son of God might obtain a spouse, towards whom he might fully exercise the infinite benevolence of his nature, and to whom he might, as it were, open and pour forth all that immense fountain of condescension, love and grace that was in his heart, and that in this way God might be glorified.[15]

Similarly, the medieval writer Hugh of St Victor wrote, 'God is preparing your soul to be a bridal chamber for Christ to dwell in.'[16] This conveys the same sentiment regarding God's purpose for his people in his Son.

That is what you and I were made for: to be known and loved by Jesus and to know and love him into all eternity, to be his inheritance, his bride and his passion. If there was no creation, God couldn't do that. If there were no undeserving, sinful people, God couldn't show grace. And so a universe is made, a universe falls and through Jesus a universe is redeemed.

Knowing that makes you very significant indeed!

Questions for reflection and discussion

- If only created things have meaning, what difference should knowing Jesus as our Creator make?
- How should the challenge of not being satisfied with 'Christ-lets' move us to seek an enlarged vision of Christ?
- How will belief in the future 'divine wedding' affect your priorities, values and discipleship today?

---

15 *The Works of Jonathan Edwards*, Vol. 13: *The 'Miscellanies'* (ed. Thomas A. Schafer; New Haven, CN: Yale University Press, 1994), p. 372, Misc. no. 271.
16 Boyd Taylor Coolman, *The Theology of Hugh of St Victor: An Interpretation* (Cambridge: Cambridge University Press, 2010), p. 27.

Prayer

O Lord, heavenly Father,
In whom is the fullness of light and wisdom,
Enlighten our minds by thy Holy Spirit,
And give us grace to receive thy Word
With reverence and humility,
Without which no man can understand thy truth,
For Christ's sake.
Amen.
(John Calvin)

3
God's full revelation (Heb. 1:3)

One of the most pernicious ideas that has spread throughout the West and which has led many people not to take Christianity seriously is that God is no more than a projection of the human mind, a form of wish fulfilment and therefore an illusion. Although the philosophical basis for this was given by the nineteenth-century German philosopher Ludwig von Feuerbach, who said, 'Man – this is the mystery of religion – projects his being into objectivity, and then again makes himself an object to this projected image of himself thus converted into a subject . . . God is the highest subjectivity of man abstracted from himself',[1] it was Sigmund Freud, the father of psychoanalysis, who gave this idea widespread popularity. In his book *The Future of an Illusion* he said that religious beliefs are 'illusions, fulfilments of the oldest, strongest and most urgent wishes of mankind . . . Thus the benevolent rule of divine Providence allays our fears of the dangers of life.'[2] In effect he was saying that the belief that there is a good, all-powerful Being in control of the world is no more than a glorified comfort blanket. It is as useful and as misleading as when a child thinks that by virtue of having a blanket to cling to and a thumb to suck on, all is right with the world, whilst all the time there is a wolf

---

1 Cited in Rodney Stark and Roger Finke, *Acts of Faith: Explaining the Human Side of Religion* (Berkeley: University of California Press, 2000), p. 1.
2 Cited in Os Guinness, *Long Journey Home* (Colorado Springs: Water Brook Press; New York: Doubleday, 2001), p. 133.

outside the door! No, says Freud, let's recognize religious belief for what it is – an illusion – and grow up.

Freud went even further. He said that many psychological illnesses, what he called 'neuroses', could be traced back to the repressive hold religious beliefs had on people's lives. In other words, religious beliefs were positively harmful, more akin to having a comfort blanket which was infected with anthrax! This was especially linked with a problem some of his patients exhibited in what he called a 'father complex'. Freud wrote that there was an 'intimate connection between the father complex and belief in God'. He stated how psychoanalysis shows 'that the personal god is logically *nothing but* an exalted father, and daily demonstrates to us how youthful persons lose their religious beliefs as soon as the authority of the father breaks down'.[3] That is to say, when young people come to the age when they realize that their fathers have faults, and feel a sense of deep disappointment and resentment as a result, that same feeling is then transferred to their belief in God. It is like realizing that Father Christmas doesn't exist after all, although the belief served a purpose while you were young and gullible.

Of course, Freud's argument can be turned back on him and other atheists like him. His argument is that our experience of a *good* father causes us to project this idea into a belief that there is a *heavenly* father – a God. But it could be that the atheists' *bad* experiences of *their* fathers have led them to *reject* belief in God. Indeed, this seems to have been the case. In his book *Faith of the Fatherless*, the writer Dr Paul Vitz has shown that all the leading world atheists – Nietzsche, Hume, Russell, Hitler, Stalin, Sartre, even Freud – had problems with their

---

3 Sigmund Freud, 'Leonardo da Vinci and a Memory of His Childhood', in *Complete Psychological Works*, vol. 11 (London: Hogarth Press, 1953), p. 123.

fathers on this score. He concludes that in example after example, 'We find weak, dead, or abusive fathers in every case.'[4] So what did they do? They linked their experiences of their fathers with their belief in God, and just because the one was intolerable and had to go, so had the other. It wasn't that they had good *reasons* which led them to reject belief in God, but rather they had bad *experiences*.

Surely what we must do in order to establish whether there is a God and what he is like is to look at the evidence around us, not at the state of our minds within us. Just because some of us may have had abusive fathers, it does not follow that *all* fathers are abusive – or that God is. Just because there is some counterfeit currency in circulation, it doesn't mean that *all* money is fake. Indeed, without real money, fake money wouldn't work at all.

What the writer to the Hebrews does is to point to a figure in history, whose life and words can be checked out, and declare that he *is* indeed some kind of God 'projection', only not a projection of *our* ideas and wishes into the heavens, but a projection of the very character and nature of God into our world.[5] He is claiming that when we come to Jesus of Nazareth

---

4 Paul Vitz, *Faith of the Fatherless: The Psychology of Atheism* (San Francisco: Ignatius Press, 2013), p. 33.

5 'The story of Jesus is nothing other than the triune life of God projected onto our history, or enacted sacramentally in our history, so that it becomes story. I use the word "projected" in the sense that we project a film onto a screen. If it is a smooth silver screen you see the film simply in itself. If the screen is twisted in some way, you get a systematically distorted image of the film. Now imagine a film projected not on a screen but on a rubbish dump. The story of Jesus – which in its full extent is the entire Bible – is the projections of the Trinitarian life of God on the rubbish dump we have made of the world. The historical mission of Jesus is nothing other than the eternal mission of the Son from the Father; the historical outpouring of the Spirit in virtue of the passion, death, and ascension of Jesus is nothing but the eternal outpouring of the Spirit from the Father through the Son. Watching, so to say, the story of Jesus, we are watching the processions of the Trinity.' Herbert McCabe, *God Matters* (London: Continuum, 2005), p. 48.

we encounter the genuine article, someone who is absolutely, uniquely God who became a man. That thought is expressed in Hebrews 1:3: 'He is the radiance of the glory of God and the exact imprint of his nature.'

'God talk' about Jesus

We have already seen that the writer is more than hinting at the divinity of Christ. First, there was the division between the prophets in the Old Testament who spoke the words of God and the Son who *is* the Word. Second, there was the division between created things and the Creator *of* all things, and the Son is definitely placed in the latter category. But now our writer describes Jesus of Nazareth in such exalted and lofty terms that can and should *only* be used of God.

First, we are told that the Son – Jesus – is 'the radiance [*apaugasma*] of God's glory' (NIV).

For the Jew, reference to God's 'glory' would have conjured up the *shekinah* glory of the Old Testament. The word 'shekinah' itself doesn't appear in the Old Testament text, but the idea certainly does. It is a word which means 'to settle' or to 'dwell with'. In the book of Exodus, the *shekinah* glory of God appeared as a pillar of fire during the night and a glowing cloud during the day to lead the people through the wilderness. It would settle on the tabernacle when they stopped (Exod. 13:20– 22). It was this radiance which filled the temple when Solomon completed its construction as he asked God to dwell within it (2 Chr. 7). However, God's glory is more than the visible manifestation of majesty, though it includes that. It is the manifestation of God's *essential nature*, which is grace or love. I say this for two reasons.

First, when in Exodus 33 Moses asked God to show him his 'glory', God's reply was,

> 'I will make all my *goodness* pass before you and will *proclaim* before you my *name* "The LORD". *And I will be gracious to whom I will be gracious, and will show mercy on whom I will show mercy.* But,' he said, 'you cannot see my face, for man shall not see me and live.'
> (Exod. 33:19–20).

Moses asks to *see* God's *glory*, and what God *proclaims* to him is his *name* which is God's goodness showing itself in mercy and grace. Certainly there is some physical manifestation, but the heart of God's glory – what his glory *is* – is grace and mercy.

Second, when John speaks of God's glory coming to dwell amongst mankind in Jesus (again the idea of the *shekinah*) he says,

> For the law was given through Moses: *grace and truth* came through Jesus Christ. No one has ever *seen* God, *but* the one and only Son, who is himself God and is in the closest relationship with the Father, *has made him known.*
> (John 1:17–18 NIV)

What is the glory of God we see in Jesus, his radiance? It is grace and truth. That is the *kind* of God he is; *that* is his glory.

The writer to the Hebrews is saying something similar here. He speaks of the *radiance* of God's glory in Jesus. This could be understood in one of two ways.

It could be passive, meaning that when the Son became a man in the incarnation, he somehow *reflected* God's glory just as a mirror reflects an image or the moon reflects the light of the sun. As you look at the moon and see its light, you are not seeing *moon*light at all; it is the *sun's* light but coming to you indirectly, reflected from the moon's surface. Some argue that it is like that when we think of the relationship between God the Father and God the Son – Jesus. In a kind of 'second-hand' way we have access to God's glory; what we see reflected in the person of Christ is genuinely of God, 'godlight', just as the moon genuinely reflects sunlight.

The other way to think of this is as something *active*, which is how most of the early church understood it. This understanding underscores the inseparable *unity* between God the Father and God the Son. According to this way of thinking, the Son is the 'radiance of God's glory' in the same way that it is not possible to imagine a lamp being lit without the filament glowing or the sun shining without its rays radiating. The two always go together; they are of the same essence. So it is here. Jesus is co-eternal with God the Father. There never was a time when the Father existed without the Son. God cannot be glorious without Christ being there, for he *is* the radiance of his glory.

This is how one Christian leader, Gregory of Nyssa (*c*.335 – 395), commented on what the writer to the Hebrews is saying:

> The majesty of the Father is expressly imaged in the greatness and power of the Son, that the one may be believed to be as great as the other is known to be. Again, as the radiance of light sheds its brilliance from the whole of the sun's disk . . . so too all the glory which the Father has is shed from its whole by means of the brightness that comes from it, that is, by the true Light. Even as the ray is

of the sun – for there would be no ray if the sun were not – the sun is never conceived as existing by itself without the ray of brightness that is shed from it. So the apostle delivered to us the continuity and eternity of that existence which the Only Begotten has of the Father, calling the Son 'the brightness of God's glory'.[6]

If this is the correct way of reading this, then we have a clear affirmation of the Son's *eternity*. This is an amazing claim. For the Jews there was only one who was eternal: God. Even the angels were created. Therefore, you don't have to be a genius to work out the equation: God is eternal; the Son is eternal; therefore the Son is God. This is what Christians declare in the Nicene Creed: 'We believe in one Lord, Jesus Christ, the only Son of God, *eternally begotten* of the Father, *God from God, Light from Light, true God from true God*, begotten, not made, of *one* Being with the Father.'

But just in case we are tempted to make the mistake of thinking that there is a *singular* God who sometimes appears as a Father, sometimes as a Son and sometimes as the Spirit (this is a heresy called 'modalism'), the writer to the Hebrews says something else about the Son, namely, that he is 'the exact imprint of his nature' or, as in the NIV, 'exact representation [*charaktēr*, from *charessein*, 'to scratch'] of his being [*hypostasis*]'. The idea here is that of a distinct *personhood*. That word translated 'representation' speaks of a precise copy, as when you stamp a seal in wax. So whilst sharing the divine nature with the Father, Jesus is *not* the Father, but by his own distinctive personhood nonetheless perfectly represents to us

---

6 *Against Eunomius* 8.1, in *Ancient Christian Commentary on Scripture: Hebrews* (ed. Erik M. Heen and Philip D. W. Krey; Downers Grove: InterVarsity Press, 2005), p. 10.

what the Father is like. As Kevin Vanhoozer comments on this verse,

'the exact imprint of God's very being': The Son corresponds to deity in every way except that he is the Son rather than the Father. Jesus is God's promise made good. Jesus is the truth because he is the Word that covenantally corresponds to, faithfully fits, and measures up to the reality of God. *Jesus is the truth because he communicates what God is.*[7]

This means that every aspect of the divine character is embodied in Jesus. In Jesus, do we see someone who is tender with the broken-hearted? So is the Father. In Jesus, do we see someone who is in total control over nature? So is the Father. In Jesus, do we see someone who hates sin and all that corrupts and demeans, and who is determined to do something about it? So is the Father. As the Puritan Thomas Goodwin writes, 'Christ adds not one drop of love to the Father's heart.'[8] We are not to play one off against the other in our minds, as if God the Father is a bullying God associated with the Old Testament and Jesus is the kind God we see in the New (which is another heresy called Marcionism). Whilst distinct, they are yet one in their divine nature, thought and purpose. 'Everything Jesus says, does and is reveals God. What there is in Christ is true knowledge of God.'[9]

---

7 Kevin J. Vanhoozer, 'Augustinian Inerrancy: Literal Meaning, Literal Truth, and Literal Interpretation', in J. Merrick, Stephen M. Garret and Stanley N. Gundry (eds.), *Five Views on Biblical Inerrancy*, Counterpoints: Bible and Theology (Grand Rapids: Zondervan, 2013), pp. 199–235 [217].
8 *The Works of Thomas Goodwin* (Edinburgh: James Nichol, 1861–66), 4:87.
9 Kevin J. Vanhoozer, *The Pastor as Public Theologian: Reclaiming a Lost Vision* (Grand Rapids: Baker, 2015), p. 110.

We live in a day when there is a 'dumbing down' in many walks of life, including in the area of religion. There is a tendency to reduce all religions and religious leaders to the same level. At heart, we are told, all religions are the same, the belief in some greater 'Ground of All Being', the need to love one another, and so on. But such thinking is lazy and breaks upon the rock of hard facts. Religions are manifestly *not* all the same, and Christianity stands out from all other religions in a number of different and highly significant ways, not least because however you want to put it, at rock bottom Christians claim that Jesus, who is without doubt a man, is also *God* and therefore must be *worshipped* as God. No-one has put the alternatives better than C. S. Lewis:

> There is no halfway house and there is no parallel in other religions. If you had gone to Buddha and asked him: 'Are you the son of Brahma?' he would have said, 'My son, you are still in the vale of illusion.' If you had gone to Socrates and asked, 'Are you Zeus?' he would have laughed at you. If you had gone to Mohammed and asked, 'Are you Allah?' he would first have rent his clothes and then cut your head off. If you had asked Confucius, 'Are you Heaven?' I think he would have probably replied, 'Remarks which are not in accordance with nature are in bad taste.' The idea of a great moral teacher saying what Christ said is out of the question. In my opinion, the only person who can say that sort of thing is either God or a complete lunatic suffering from that form of delusion, which undermines the whole mind of man. If you think you are a poached egg, when you are not looking for a piece of toast to suit you, you may be sane, but if you think

you are God, there is no chance for you. We may note in passing that He was never regarded as a mere moral teacher. He did not produce that effect on any of the people who actually met him. He produced mainly three effects – Hatred – Terror – Adoration. There was no trace of people expressing mild approval.[10]

Lewis is correct. Wherever you look in the Gospels, Jesus tended to produce one of those three reactions.

First, the religious authorities hated him and couldn't wait to be rid of him (Mark 3:6). This still happens today, not by hanging but by heresy: Jesus is reduced to a 'mere man for others', someone who can be revered alongside Mohammed or the Buddha. It's just another way of 'killing him', rendering him ineffective so he isn't a threat.

Several years ago, Bishop John Shelby Spong, of Newark, New Jersey, wrote a book entitled *Born of a Woman: A Bishop Rethinks the Birth of Jesus*. In this book he claims that Jesus' conception was natural, and that his mother, Mary, had probably been raped. He denies *all* the miraculous elements in the Bible and pours scorn on those who would naively (in his view) read them as history. He argues that belief in the virgin birth has led to a negative view of women and that in the end Jesus actually married Mary Magdalene. He writes:

The time has come for the church to surrender its neurotic pattern of trafficking in one feeble religious security system after another and to allow its people to feel the

---

10 C. S. Lewis, 'What Are We to Make of Jesus Christ?', in *God in the Dock* (London: Fount, 1979), pp. 79–84 [81].

bracing wind of insecurity so that Christians might know what it means to walk by faith.[11]

This bishop specialized in creating a lack of assurance – 'insecurity'. The Bible can't be trusted, with the result that faith is undermined. This stands in stark contrast to the writer to the Hebrews who, drawing Christian believers to the bedrock of their faith in the incarnation of the Son of God, encourages them to continue in it in 2:1–4:

> We must pay the most careful attention, therefore, to what we have heard, so that we do not drift away. For since the message spoken through angels was binding, and every violation and disobedience received its just punishment, how shall we escape if we ignore so great a salvation? This salvation, which was first announced by the Lord, was confirmed to us by those who heard him. God also testified to it by signs, wonders and various miracles, and by gifts of the Holy Spirit distributed according to his will.
>
> (NIV)

The second response to Jesus was that some were genuinely terrified. This was the case with his disciples on more than one occasion as, for example, after the stilling of the storm; the disciples knew from their Scriptures that only *God* could do such a thing, yet here was someone in the boat with them who had just done it. They turned pale with fear (Ps. 89; cf. Mark 4:35–41).

---

11 John Shelby Spong, *Born of a Woman: A Bishop Rethinks the Birth of Jesus* (San Francisco: HarperSanFrancisco, 1992), p. 13.

Similarly, there are those who shelter behind atheism, not necessarily because they believe it to be a viable intellectual option, but because of the fear that if Jesus is who the Bible claims he is, then their lifestyle will have to change. In a startling moment of candour the atheist Aldous Huxley confessed,

> For myself, no doubt, as for many of my contemporaries, the philosophy of meaninglessness was essentially liberation from a certain political and economic system and liberation from a certain system of morality. We objected to the morality because it interfered with our sexual freedom; we objected to the political and economic system because it was unjust. The supporters of these systems claimed that in some way they embodied the meaning (a Christian meaning they insisted) of the world. There was one admirably simple method of confuting these people and at the same time justifying ourselves in our political and erotic revolt: We could deny that the world had any meaning whatsoever.[12]

The third response to Jesus was adoration. This was the response of 'Doubting' Thomas when the penny finally dropped about the person of Jesus. As he met the risen Lord he simply fell on his knees and exclaimed, 'My Lord and my *God!*' (John 20:28). That is what you are meant to do when you encounter God: worship.

Which of these three reactions characterizes your attitude towards Jesus? Do you hate him, fear him or simply adore him

---

12 Aldous Huxley, *Ends and Means* (London: Chatto & Windus, 1946), p. 273.

as the one who is God? Putting it bluntly, if you don't know Jesus, you simply don't know God. As John Calvin wrote,

God so proclaims himself the sole God as to offer himself to be contemplated clearly as three persons. Unless we grasp these, only the bare and empty name of God flits about in our brains, to the exclusion of the true God.[13]

Professor Thomas Torrance spelled out the implications in a way which borders on the poetic:

There is in fact no God behind the back of Jesus, no act of God other than the act of Jesus, no God but the God we see and meet in him. Jesus Christ is the open heart of God, the very love and life of God poured out to redeem humankind, the mighty hand and power of God stretched out to heal and save sinners. All things are in God's hands, but the hands of God and the hands of Jesus, in life and in death, are the same.[14]

Jesus Christ *is* the open heart of God as well as the 'human face' of God.

Questions for reflection and discussion

- In the light of what the writer to the Hebrews says about Jesus being the 'radiance of God's glory' and the 'exact representation of his being', how might we understand Jesus'

---

13 John Calvin, *Institutes of the Christian Religion*, 2 vols. (ed. John T. McNeill; trans. Ford Lewis Battles; Philadelphia: Westminster, 1960), 1:13.2.
14 Thomas F. Torrance, 'The Christ Who Loves Us', in Thomas F. Torrance, James B. Torrance and David W. Torrance (eds.), *A Passion for Christ: The Vision that Ignites Ministry* (Eugene: Wipf & Stock, 2010), pp. 9–22 [17].

statement 'Anyone who has seen me has seen the Father' (John 14:9 NIV)?

- Of the three common reactions to Christ in the Bible, which one best reflects your attitude? Does it do justice to God's self-revelation in his Son?
- What differences does looking on the 'human face of God' make to your devotion to God and your explaining of God to others?

Prayer

Grant me, even me, my dearest Lord, to know thee and
rejoice in thee.
And if I cannot do these perfectly in this life, let me at least
advance to higher degrees every day, till I can come to do
them in perfection. Let the knowledge of thee increase
In me here, that it may be full hereafter.
Let the love of thee grow every day more and more here,
That it may be perfect hereafter;
That my joy may be great in itself, and full in thee.
I know, O God, that thou art a god of truth,
O make good thy gracious promises to me,
That my joy may be full.
Amen.
(St Augustine of Hippo)

4

God's fitting sacrifice (Heb. 1:3)

It had been an especially tiring day for the prison psychiatrist. With more than a hint of despair in his voice he confided in the chaplain: 'I tell you honestly Reverend; I can cure somebody's madness but I can do nothing about his badness.' 'Psychiatry', he went on, 'properly administered can turn a schizophrenic bank robber into a mentally healthy bank robber. A good teacher can turn an illiterate criminal into an educated criminal. But they are still bank robbers and criminals.'[1]

You have to admire that psychiatrist for his honesty as well as empathize with him in his despondency. He did, however, draw a very important distinction, namely, that *treating* people is one thing, but *curing* them is something else.

It is not easy being diagnosed with an illness when you least expect it. I remember when my grandad, who, for most of his eighty or so years had hardly had a day's illness, was told he was suffering from diabetes. Grandad was always one for the home-made remedy. When I was little I cut my finger, and his solution was to get out the salt pot and pour salt onto the gaping wound (well, it seemed gaping to me at the time)! When I had a loose tooth, his remedy was straightforward and crude: one end of a thread was attached to the tooth and the other to a door handle; as the door was slammed shut, out came the tooth, flying across

---

1 Charles Colson and Nancy Pearcey, *A Dangerous Grace: Daily Readings* (Waco: Word, 1994), p. 123.

the room! However, he could apply no such remedy to his diabetes. Today diabetes can be treated but not cured. What's the difference between a treatment and a cure? It is this: the treatment has to *continually* be applied, whereas a cure has a certain finality about it. The daily administration of insulin can keep the illness under control, but it can never be relaxed as otherwise the illness will take over.

The writer to the Hebrews is saying something similar about the nature of Old Testament religion – or of any religion for that matter – namely, that all we find there is but a temporary treatment, keeping in check the spiritual problem of sin and its disastrous effects in terms of our relationship with God and one another. By way of contrast, Jesus has come not to tender a treatment but to effect a cure.

Although the rest of the letter, especially chapters 9 and 10, explains *how* this is so, it is highlighted right at the very beginning in this prologue at the end of verse 3: 'After making *purification for sins*, he [Jesus] sat down at the right hand of the Majesty on high.'

The centrality of the cure

We have been seeing how in many different ways our writer has been highlighting the divine identity of Jesus. He is God's Son, not just a prophet; he is the world's Creator and Sustainer – sole functions of God. But now we come to something else which the Jews ascribed only to God: the one true God is not only the world's Ruler, he alone is the world's Redeemer – that is *who* God is.

You see this repeated over and over again in the book of Isaiah, for example. Not only is Yahweh the great Creator

(Isa. 40), but he is also the great Redeemer who has a set purpose of rescuing his people:

> Remember the former things, those of long ago;
>> I am God, and there is no other;
>> I am God; and there is none like me.
>
> (Isa. 46:9 NIV)

He then goes on to relate how he is going to bring about the salvation of his people:

> I am bringing my righteousness near,
>> it is not far away;
>> and my salvation will not be delayed.
> I will grant salvation to Zion,
>> my splendour to Israel.
>
> (46:13 NIV)

Here in Hebrews 1:3 we see that *Jesus* (whose name means 'The Lord saves') is the one who rescues his people. The divine identity of Jesus as Lord/Yahweh of the Old Testament is underscored again: God is Ruler; Jesus is Ruler; therefore Jesus is God. God is Rescuer; Jesus is Rescuer; therefore Jesus is God.

It doesn't show itself that clearly in our English translations, but the notion that the completion of Jesus' work is evidenced by his exaltation is conveyed by the writer using a literary device called a 'chiasmus',[2] whereby the verses are arranged in an inverted parallel structure focusing on a central point:

---

2 Victor (Sung-Yul) Rhee, 'Chiasm and Its Christological Implication in Hebrews 1:1–14', *Journal of Biblical Literature* 131 (2012), pp. 341–362.

A. Function of the Son: God's final spokesman (1:1–2a)

  B. Son in his exaltation: heir of all things (1:2b)

    C. Son in his pre-existence: bearer of God's nature,
Creator and Sustainer of the world (1:2c–3b)

      D. Son in his incarnation: purifier of sins (1:3c)

        *E. Son in his exaltation: he has sat down at
the right hand of God, with the result that
he became superior to the angels (1:3d–4)*

        *E'. Son in his exaltation: because of the
Father's instalment at the right hand,
he is superior to the angels (1:5)*

      D'. Son in his incarnation: as the firstborn,
he is superior to the angels (1:6)

    C'. Son in his pre-existence: the Son is superior
to angels because he is God (1:7–12)

  B'. Son in his exaltation: the Son is superior to the
angels because the Father has exalted him in his
right hand (1:13)

A'. Function of the angels: the Son is superior to the angels
because the angels are the ministering spirits for the
sons who will inherit salvation (1:14)[3]

The question arises: what does the Son rescue us from? The
answer is: the effects of sin.

The nature of the cure

The writer speaks of 'purification for sins'. This tells us something about what sin *is*: it is a moral pollutant. Like some filthy,

---

3 Rhee, 'Chiasm', pp. 1–2.

foul-smelling chemical in the air, it seeps into every pore and crevice, blocking up the lungs, clogging the arteries, until it finally overwhelms and kills us. However, sin isn't as passive as that: those are its effects, but it is also linked to *our own moral choices*. In this sense it is more like us *welcoming* the pollutant and not worrying about the consequences. Worse than that, it is us thinking that the chemicals will actually do us good and so we want more and more (later the author speaks of the 'fleeting *pleasures* of sin', 11:24–26). Sin is a kind of madness. It is so serious that we need purifying from it before it ultimately destroys us eternally.

This is why the Son became incarnate, a man, and why his death is absolutely central to all that Christians believe. The person of Christ (God incarnate) cannot be separated from the purpose of Christ (the redemption of sinners).

For centuries the Jews had been carefully schooled by God that before sin could be forgiven a sacrifice had to be offered. The blood spread on the surface of the altar symbolized in the most vivid terms the appalling penalty that sin demands: death (see Lev. 16). God cannot ignore sin; for him to do so would be tantamount to him abdicating his role as the moral ruler of the universe, which he cannot do. Sin has to be punished; wrongdoing demands a penalty. If there is any doubt in our minds about that claim, how would we feel if, after the horrors of Auschwitz had been uncovered, the judges at Nuremberg had simply said to the Nazis on trial, 'What a pity – of course, you have been led astray by your ideology. Now run along, and don't do it again'? There is such a thing as *natural law*, written on the heart of every man and woman, and integral to that moral sense we all have is that justice has to be done. God would agree; after all, he was the one who wrote that law into our hearts in the first place, reflecting something of his own moral character. God can no more ignore your misdoings or mine than we can ignore each other's. Sin brings with it a penalty: death (Heb. 9:27). This is the consistent witness of the whole of the Old Testament. Examples such as Numbers 14:34; 30:15; Lamentations 5:7; and Ezekiel 4:4–5 led John Stott to conclude that

> It is clear from Old Testament usage that to 'bear sin' means neither to sympathise with sinners, nor to identify with their pain, nor to express their penitence, nor to be persecuted on account of human sinfulness (as others have argued), nor even to suffer the consequences of sin in personal or social terms, but specifically to endure its penal consequences, to undergo its penalty.[4]

The slaughter of an animal on the altar was for a Jew not only a graphic reminder of the penalty for sin, it was also a moving picture of the mercy of God. This was God's way of ensuring that those who put their trust in him could be accepted by him, since God treated the animal as if it were the guilty sinner; he graciously accepted the animal in the place of the offending party. In short, this was a *substitutionary* sacrifice. This is what the writer to the Hebrews goes on to describe at length in chapters 9 and 10. The fact that sacrifices had to be made, day after day, month after month, year upon year, simply served to underscore their provisionality; they were a treatment, not a cure.

When the Son of God came into the world, all of that was to change.

---

4 John R. W. Stott, *The Cross of Christ* (Leicester: Inter-Varsity Press, 1986), p. 143.

The incarnation was necessary because only flesh can die; only a body can be pierced and bleed.[5] What is more, only a *person* can voluntarily offer himself as a sacrifice on behalf of others. The sheep being slaughtered in the temple couldn't do that: all they could do was bleat; but the Son *says* to his Father, 'Here I am, Father, I will go and die for them. I will lay down my life so that they may live. I will shed my pure blood so that they can be made clean, because we love them, Father, and they can't save themselves. In fact, Father, this is why we made a world: so that we could share our eternal love with people like these' (Heb. 10:5–7).

Here and here alone is the cure for sin and not merely a treatment: the divine remedy which totally expunges our moral guilt once and for all. Like a magnet, the dirty iron filings of our sin are drawn into God incarnate's perfect, sinless body. The blood of goats is set aside for the blood of the Son. The penalty for sin is paid, the power of sin is subdued, and one day in glory the presence of sin will be no more.

Many people in our society are just plain tired. Not just tired of the daily grind of work and the lack of purpose and direction in life, but tired of the weariness that sin and guilt produce. At some point everyone has a troubled conscience. There are things we do and have done which simply cut us to the heart and we feel that it would be like dying a thousand deaths if those closest to us knew what we were truly like and what we had really done. Perhaps more than that, the tiredness springs ultimately from being cut off from the Giver of life – God – because we simply can't bear the thought of facing *him* with our guilt. Like Adam and Eve, we would prefer to run away and

---

5 See Stephen Motyer, 'Not Apart From Us (Hebrews 11:40): Physical Community in the Letter to the Hebrews', *Evangelical Quarterly* 77.3 (2005), pp. 235–247.

hide, or to distract ourselves, rather than find ourselves alone with our guilt before our Maker.

But it needn't be so – not now, because Jesus has made purification for our sins. Just as when you press the 'delete' button on your computer and the page becomes blank, so as we turn to Jesus, confessing our need and casting ourselves on his tender mercy, the 'delete' button is pressed and our sin in God's sight vanishes:

> I, I am he
> who blots out your transgressions for my own sake,
> and I will not remember your sins.
> (Isa. 43:25)

How can we be certain that this is so? We can be sure because Jesus has '*sat down* at the right hand of the Majesty in heaven' (NIV). In the Old Testament temple the priest had to keep standing because his work was never finished – there was always one more goat to kill, one more bull to slaughter; but not any more. There is no further sacrifice required: Jesus has paid it all, and so he can sit down to rule having been crucified to redeem.

Notice, too, *where* he sits: 'at the right hand of the Majesty on high'. He sits on the heavenly throne, which means that he is now ruling the world as *a man* with the Father.

Taking the finished work to God

It is possible to stop short in recognizing the full nature of Christ's atoning work. By that I mean that we do not always follow the writer to the Hebrews through in seeing how Christ's finished work achieved on the cross as a 'purification for sins' is taken into *heaven* so that its benefits can be eternally enjoyed by believers.

This is where the doctrine of the ascension plays its part: 'sitting at the right hand of God'.

The tabernacle built by Moses and the temple later built by Solomon were only 'shadows' or copies of the heavenly realities which Christ revealed and into which he has now entered (Heb. 8:5). Contrasting what Aaron as high priest had to do with what Christ as *the* High Priest has done, the writer to the Hebrews says,

> But when Christ appeared as a high priest of the good things that have come, then through the greater and more perfect tent (not made with hands, that is, not of this creation) he entered once for all into the holy places, not by means of the blood of goats and calves but by means of his own blood, thus securing an eternal redemption . . . For Christ has entered, not into holy places made with hands, which are copies of the true things, but into heaven itself, now to appear in the presence of God on our behalf. (9:11–12, 24)

Gerrit Scott Dawson describes the theological and spiritual entailments of what Hebrews is depicting in this way:

> Having made a perfect sacrifice, it was time for Jesus to take his offering into the Holy of Holies. Clad now in his priestly garment of glorified flesh, humanity in its fullest, restored unto eternal life, Jesus ascended into the Most Holy Place. So Jesus in his ascension took the offering of

his blood into the true Holy of Holies, the presence of his Father. In our name and on our behalf, he offered his perfect obedience. In our stead, he offered his sacrifice. And it was accepted. Unlike Aaron, however, Jesus has not yet returned to his people waiting outside. He remains inside 'the inner sanctuary behind the curtain' (Hebrews 6:19). There he continues to intercede for us (Hebrews 7:25), and though he has not yet returned in the flesh to bring the time of consummation, he still blesses us . . . the ascended Christ receives the Holy Spirit from his father and pours him out upon the disciples. The blessing, the Spirit, imprints the name and identity of God upon us in an even more potent and dynamic way than the wonderful Aaronic blessing ever could.[6]

Talk about a cure!

The benefits of the cure

We are in deep and mysterious territory, but what we need to grasp is that as a result of God the Son becoming a man, dying a man's death and ascending back into heaven as a man, a change has been introduced into God: 'flesh and blood has been taken into the deity'.[7] If I can reverently put it this way: as a result of the incarnation and atonement (Jesus dying, rising and ascending for us), God will never be the same again. What is more, our relationship with him will never be the same again: it will be infinitely better.

---

6 Gerrit Scott Dawson, *Jesus Ascended: The Meaning of Christ's Continuing Incarnation* (Edinburgh: T&T Clark, 2004), p. 122.
7 Motyer, 'Not Apart From Us', p. 238.

What does this truth guarantee?

First, it means that God is able to *sympathize with us*. One writer describes it like this:

Let us never imagine that God does not understand us. God's Son took our nature. He entered our experience. He knows what physical pain is. He knows what emotional and spiritual pain is. He knows what the loss of God is. He stood in the outer darkness: in the place where there is no comfort; in the place of the absolute 'Why?' where, needing God as no man ever needed God, He cried and God was not there. Bearing a burden such as the world has never known, and left comfortless. We never go beyond his pain. Our darkness is never more intense than his. Our 'Why's' are never more bewildered. Sometimes, when we ask, 'Why me?' part of His answer is, 'Me too!'[8]

As the writer to the Hebrews goes on to say, 'For we do not have a high priest who is unable to feel sympathy for our weaknesses, but we have one who has been tempted in every way, just as we are – yet he did not sin' (4:15 NIV).

Second, related to this, it means that God will always be *well disposed towards us*. It doesn't follow from that that everything is going to be easy, but it does mean that whatever happens, God will always have a good purpose in it (Rom. 8:28). Even when we sin, because of what Jesus has done for us on the cross to purify us, God doesn't look on us in the same way he did before we trusted Christ. Then he was a judge towards us, with his law set over and against us; now he is our loving Father,

---

8 Donald Macleod, *A Faith to Live By: Understanding Christian Doctrine* (Fearn, Ross-shire: Mentor, 1998), p. 123.

with his Son rooting for us. Because Jesus has gone into heaven, he looks down from heaven like a kindly, sympathetic older brother whose heart goes out towards us in compassion, not anger; how could it be otherwise, as he has already suffered God's anger for our sin on our behalf on the cross?

This is one of the richest blessings which result from Christ's atoning work and *continuing* incarnation.

Let me end with an example of this life-transforming truth that Christ purifies us from our sins.

Odessa Moore was a Christian prison visitor in the USA. She met a teenager who was waiting to be tried for first degree murder. When Odessa met him, his eyes were filled with nothing but hate. As they talked, the all-too-familiar story began to emerge: father a drug addict, mother an alcoholic, and both would beat the boy and lock him in a cupboard for hours on end. All his life he had been fed the line that he was nothing. 'But that was all right,' he said, 'because I don't care for nobody.' 'But there is someone who loves you,' responded Odessa. However, he refused point-blank to believe it.

'Look,' said Odessa eventually, 'you are here for murder, right?'

'Yes, and I would do it again,' he said.

'Well,' Odessa continued, 'how would you like it if someone came here tonight and said, "I know you have committed murder and that you are going to get the death penalty, but I am here to take your place." How would you like that?'

Now she had his attention, and for the first time his eyes showed a spark of life. 'Are you kidding!' he gasped. 'That would be great.' So she went on to tell him about Jesus who became the scapegoat who had already died to take his place, who had paid the price already. Step by step she took him through the gospel until at the end of the evening the stone-cold teenager had melted, weeping tears of repentance as he committed his life to Christ. He knew what he needed – forgiveness – and he knew he did not have it within himself but that God did, so he reached out and received it. Then his standing before God as a forgiven son was certain.[9]

Jesus is the God who made us and for whom we were made. Jesus is the God who became one of us in order to redeem us and who is kindly disposed towards us. Jesus, God incarnate, is the one who is to capture our hearts, our imaginations and our lives, because he came, not to offer a treatment, but to bring a cure.

Questions for reflection and discussion

- How would you describe the nature of sin and God's 'cure' according to Hebrews?
- When you feel cast down because of failures caused by sin, how will knowing that Christ became one of us who can sympathize with us help you?
- How does understanding God's changed attitude towards you because of Jesus change your attitude towards God?

Prayer

The gift of thy only-begotten Son Jesus Christ our Lord,
Whom thou gavest for us
To be our Saviour, our Redeemer, our Peace-maker,
Our Wisdom, our Sanctification, and our Righteousness,
Is the most excellent gift and most precious treasure!
Wonderfully, O most loving Father,

---

9 Colson and Pearcey, *Dangerous Grace*, p. 110.

Doth this thing set forth thy hearty love toward us,
That when we were yet ungodly and wicked sinners,
Thou gavest thy Son to die for our sins.
Amen.
(Thomas Brown)

5

God's fullness of being
(Heb. 1:5–14)

Have you ever seen an angel? That is, a real one, not some cute child who will run errands for you or who appears on the stage at the school nativity? I can't say I have, although according to the writer to the Hebrews I may have done, because he tells us that Christians have shown kindness to angels without even realizing it (13:2). I assume that angels are therefore in disguise, taking human form, because there is no way you wouldn't know that you had 'entertained' an angel if one had come knocking at the door with wings unfurled! I have never seen an angel in, if you like, its full naked 'angelness', because if I had I certainly would remember it.

However, the picture we are given of angels in the Bible is not at all like the Botticelli cherubs with fat pink tummies; rather, they are fiery, fearsome creatures who are able to stand in the presence of God without being consumed. The reason I can say that they are fearsome is because whenever angels appear in the Gospels, the first words they seem to say to their startled audience are 'Don't be afraid' (Luke 1:13, 30; 2:10), and they wouldn't have to say that if they were of the Botticelli cherub variety!

But you may be thinking to yourself, 'That is all well and good, but angels don't seem to figure all that much in a person's thinking today.' I myself might have said this at one time – until, that is, I looked at the books being sold on the subject in one of our well-known high street bookshops. There I found titles such as *Angels in America* – a two-part drama epic set during the Reagan years; *Big book of Angel Tarot*; *The Night the Angels Came*; *Angel Fever*; *Angels on Assignment*; *Ask Your Angels*; *Angelic Healing*; *Angelic Voices*; *Angels: An Endangered Species*. Angels and angelology appear to be big business.

What may come as a surprise is the way the writer to the Hebrews suddenly appears to switch direction with all this talk of angels, or, to be more precise, with feeling the need to convince his readers that Jesus is superior to angels. We have seen how within the short space of four verses our author has already crammed in heaps of teaching about Jesus' divinity: that he is the Creator, Sustainer and Redeemer of the universe – roles reserved solely for Israel's God – and so it would seem to be redundant, to say the least, to have to prove that he is bigger and better than angels. Of course he is if he is God! But for some reason the writer is compelled to underscore the point, as we see in 1:4: 'So he became *as much superior* to the angels as the name he has inherited is superior to theirs' (NIV). He then spends the next *ten* verses demonstrating Christ's undeniable superiority to angelic beings by drawing on a catena (Hebrew *ḥărûzîm*, 'string of pearls') of Old Testament quotations. Again he will show plainly that the Son, although human, is divine. Angels, we are told, worship the Son (v. 6). The Son does not worship angels.

We may think that this is rather 'over the top'. Was our writer somehow anticipating the renewed interest in angels in the first part of the twenty-first century, so wanting to put them in their place? No. What our writer wants to do is to put Jesus firmly in *his* place by putting the most exalted, awesome creatures ever conceived in *their* place – namely, *below* him.

But there may have been another reason why the author went to such great lengths to establish beyond a shadow of a doubt that Christ is not inferior to angels, and that is because there *was* a time in history when he became just that: inferior, in the sense that by virtue of becoming human he occupied a lower place in creation's order. That is what the author goes on to say in chapter 2 as he quotes Psalm 8 and applies it to Jesus: 'But', he writes, 'we do see Jesus, who *was made lower than the angels for a little while*, now crowned with glory and honour because he suffered death' (2:9 NIV). One could therefore imagine some people thinking that, whereas at 'one time' the Son may have been all the things the writer has been speaking about, now, as a result of the incarnation, his status has diminished so that he is not even as mighty as the angels. Our writer, however, won't allow such a thought to be entertained even for a moment. He does this by making a contrast between Jesus who *was* lower than the angels for a period of time by virtue of his incarnation, and Jesus who is *now* superior to the angels by virtue of his redeeming work. This is precisely the central point made in the 'chiasmus' of 1:3b–4: 'After making purification for sins, he sat down at the right hand of the Majesty on high, *having* become as much superior to angels as the name he has inherited is more excellent than theirs.'

The author wants to establish in the minds and hearts of his readers that Jesus has always been and will always be superior to *every* creature because he is one with the God of Israel, the Creator, even though he has now taken humanity into the Godhead: Jesus is the God-*man*.[1]

---

1 See Richard Bauckham, 'The Divinity of Jesus in the Letter to the Hebrews', in *Jesus and the God of Israel: 'God Crucified' and Other Essays on the New Testament's Christology of Divine Identity* (Grand Rapids: Eerdmans, 2008), pp. 233–253.

If there is a hierarchy within creation, ranging from the angels at the top of the scale, who are 'ministering spirits' (v. 14), to human beings, who are 'a little lower than the angels' (Ps. 8:5 NIV), then while Jesus for a period of thirty years or so was at the lower end of the scale, he has now changed the order of things, having become a human while never ceasing to be God, so that now *humanity* has been exalted *above* the angels *in him*.[2] Even the 'world to come', mentioned in Hebrews 2:5, is subject to Jesus, and this will include angels. By Jesus becoming a human and dying for humans, he has changed the status of humans, such that for Christians the angels become *their* servants: 'Are not all angels ministering spirits sent to *serve those who will inherit salvation*?' (1:14 NIV).

One of the main themes of this letter is the superiority (*kreitton*) of the Son. As we have seen, he is superior to the best of the priests the Levitical order could provide, and offers a superior sacrifice to that prescribed by the law of Moses, which leads to a better country shaped by better promises. As Graham Cole observes, 'Jewish Christians in danger of letting go their Christian distinctives in the face of outside pressures needed to be reminded of this superiority and should not drift from the message they had first embraced (Heb. 2:1).'[3] Now he demonstrates the Son's 'higher ranking' (*kreitton*) over angelic beings.

The structure of this introduction to Hebrews (what is technically called an 'exordium') has been helpfully laid out by

---

2 Paul speaks of Christians already being seated with Christ in the heavenly realms (Eph. 2:6), and in 1 Cor. 6:3 he says that Christians will 'judge angels', suggesting superiority over them.

3 Graham A. Cole, *The God Who Became Human: A Biblical Theology of the Incarnation*, New Studies in Biblical Theology (Leicester: Apollos, 2013), p. 105.

Richard Bauckham,[4] underscoring the author's belief that the Son is to be identified with the God of Israel:

A Son,

Whom he appointed heir of *all things*,	(1) Eschatological rule over all things (Ps. 2:8; 8:6)
Through whom he also created *the worlds.*	(2) Agent of creation of all things
Being the reflection of God's glory and the exact imprint of God's very being,	(3) Eternal divine being (cf. Wis. 7:26)
Sustaining *all things* by his powerful word,	(4) Providential sovereignty over all things
Having made purification for sins,	(5) High priestly atonement
He *sat down* at the right hand of the majesty *on high*	(6) Exaltation to God's throne in heaven (Ps. 110:1)
Having become as much *superior to angels* as the name he has inherited is more excellent than theirs	(7) Identification (name) as YHWH

Let's now see how the writer demonstrates, against the beliefs of the Jehovah's Witnesses and 'progressives' within the church, that Jesus is, has always been and will always be uniquely God, worthy of our worship and complete trust.

---

4 Bauckham, 'Divinity of Jesus', p. 238.

What's in a name?

First, Jesus is superior because of *his name*: 'having become as much superior to angels as the name he has inherited is more excellent than theirs' (1:4). What does the writer mean by Jesus 'inheriting a name'? The 'Name' for the Jew was the unique name of God revealed to Moses, which is 'YHWH', 'I AM WHO I AM' (Exod. 3:14). This is the *personal* name which belongs to the Father, and it is also a name which belongs by rights to Jesus, as the Father's Son. Once Jesus had completed the work on earth he was sent to do – namely, to offer himself as a sacrifice for sin – then, on being exalted to the right hand of God, 'the Majesty in heaven' (NIV), he took his rightful place to rule as the God-man, and so the name which belongs to the Father, 'I AM', also properly belongs to him. God the Father is the self-existent one and Ruler over all – the 'I AM' – and so is the Son. You can't say that of any being in creation, not even one so exalted as the archangel Gabriel! Angels were created; the Son is the self-existent 'I AM'. The sixteenth-century theologian John Calvin stressed that there was no *essential* subordination of the Son to the Father. He used the Greek term *autotheos* to underscore that Christ was God in his own right. His deity wasn't imparted, derived or dependent; it was from his very self (Latin, *a se ipso*).

Allow the magnitude of this claim to sink in.

Within forty years of Jesus walking the earth, eating fish, drinking wine, building houses – and performing the most astonishing miracles – he was being proclaimed – by *Jews* – to be 'Yahweh', 'I AM'. On one occasion Jesus claimed the 'Name' himself: 'Before Abraham was, I am,' he said (John 8:58). What was it that made the first believers engage in such a seismic shift in their thinking, doing something which a few years earlier would have been considered utterly blasphemous, namely, attributing the divine name to a Galilean? It has already been hinted at: Jesus died, rose and ascended. Jesus did 'God stuff', if you like, such as forgiving sins, calming seas, raising the dead; so what else were they to conclude, however difficult it was to get their minds around, but that *Jesus* is the great 'I AM'? And we are meant to do the same on the basis of the same evidence.

Know your place

Second, Jesus is superior because of *his position*. This comes out in a number of ways.

Hebrews chapter 1 is structured using a literary device known as an *inclusio*, whereby Psalm 110 forms the 'literary bracket' at either end. This psalm is alluded to at the beginning in verse 3, which speaks of Jesus 'sitting down at the right hand of the Majesty in heaven', and it is actually quoted at the end in verse 13:

> Sit at my right hand
> until I make your enemies a footstool for your feet.

The right hand of the Majesty in heaven is the supreme position of God's cosmic rule, past, present and future. It is the right hand which directs the course of the planets as well as the course of history. It is the right hand which lifts up rulers only to put them down again. It is the right hand which brings every individual into the world (Ps. 139), and which also takes them out of it (Ps. 90:5). It is the right hand which directs angels

where to go and what to do, not least to protect God's little ones
(Matt. 18:10), from which we get the notion of 'guardian angels'
(which also may lie behind Heb. 1:14). Furthermore, that it is
as *God* that the Son reigns from heaven is the main thrust of
Psalm 45, quoted in Hebrews 1:8:

> But about the *Son* he says,
> 　'*Your* throne, *O God*, will last for ever and ever;
> 　　a sceptre of justice will be the sceptre of your
> 　　　kingdom.
> 　You have loved righteousness and hated wickedness;
> 　　therefore God, your God, has set you above your
> 　　　companions
> 　　by anointing you with the oil of joy.'
> (NIV)

There is also further significance in God addressing the Son in
these Old Testament quotations:

> The words of the Old Testament citations might have
> been scripted centuries before, and have been spoken of
> many times in the life and worship of God's people, but
> they had an appointed time of ultimate fulfilment and
> full expression in the life of the Son. In the case of
> the Old Testament citations in Hebrews 1 the divine
> conversation they record takes place at the time of the
> enthronement of the Son on high . . . the writer presents
> the Old Testament citations in Hebrews 1 and 2 as
> offering a *window* into a *conversation* that takes place
> between *two divine persons* in the Godhead. The sig-
> nificance of the fact that God converses with the

Son through these citations should not be overlooked
[emphasis mine].[5]

Jesus the Son is now in heaven ruling. He is the one the
Puritans referred to as 'heaven's darling'. It is through God
the Son that God the Father exercises his righteous rule over
all the earth (what theologians call the 'mediatorial kingdom'[6]).

If you switch on the news to see the dreadful plight of people
subject to the ravages of war, or the thousands of women and
even children embroiled in the sex trade, or the loan sharks
who seem to be getting away with murder, quite literally in
some cases – never think that God does not care and does not
hate it. He hates it with a holy passion, and one day he will
judge it through his Son and everyone will be brought to
account: all wrongs will be righted. Jesus stood against such
things while on earth, and he is no less set against them while
in heaven but is determined to perfectly establish his reign of
righteousness.

The positional superiority of Jesus is also displayed, as we
have already seen, in terms of the spatial imagery used with the
notion of *height*. In the grand scheme of things, angels occupy
the higher echelons of the created order, such that they are
often portrayed as encircling the throne of God – as we see in
Revelation:

Then I looked and heard the voice of many *angels*,
numbering thousands upon thousands, and ten thousand
times ten thousand. They encircled the throne and the

5 Jonathan Griffiths, 'Hebrews and the Trinity', in Brandon D. Crowe and Carl R.
Trueman (eds.), *The Essential Trinity* (London: Apollos, 2016), pp. 126–127.
6 See D. A .Carson, *The Sermon on the Mount* (Grand Rapids: Baker, 1978), p. 12.

living creatures and the elders. In a loud voice they were saying:
    'Worthy is the Lamb, who was slain,
        to receive power and wealth and wisdom and
            strength
        and honour and glory and praise!'
(Rev. 5:12 NIV)

Who is it who is receiving the praise of these higher order of beings? In Revelation 4 it is God the Father; in Revelation 5 it is the Lamb – God the Son.

Perhaps we can think of it this way: to be above the angels is to be God; to be below the angels is to be human. Where is Jesus now? He is above the angels *as* a human! Everything has changed as a result of Christ's death and resurrection.

The same point is made in Hebrews 1:6 with the quotation from Deuteronomy 32:43: 'Let all God's angels *worship* him' – speaking of the Son. Angels don't worship angels. Angels certainly don't worship human beings. Angels worship *God*, and here we are told that they are exhorted to worship Jesus.

Let's try to grasp something of the breathtaking significance of this.

There is now a *human being* on the throne of the universe. In the place of supreme and central significance of all creation there is a man, a member of, and the head of, the human race, in a way God had intended all along (Ps. 8; Heb. 2:5–9). If you were to go to the place where angels who never fell engage in endless worship, you will find a man. Go to the very centre of the manifestation of the invisible God and you will find a man whose true human nature shines with the holiness of God, so that all the angels and all the creatures fall on their faces and cry 'Glory!' If angels do that, how much more should we? The angels have the delight and privilege of worshipping the Son as their Creator; Christians have the additional delight and privilege of worshipping him as their Redeemer.

'This is my Son'

Third, Jesus is superior by virtue of *his sonship*. God has never said to any angel that which he has said to the one who in history became the man Jesus:

> For to which of the angels did God ever say,
>   'You are my Son,
>   today I have begotten you'?
> Or again,
>   'I will be to him a father,
>   and he shall be to me a son'?
> (1:5)

Here we have two quotes about the Messiah, one from Psalm 2, the other from 2 Samuel 7:14. Don't be thrown by the time reference, '*today* I have begotten you' (or 'become your Father', NIV), as if there was a time when Jesus was *not* the Son of God (the heresy of Arius). In this case, the imagery being used is that of God's king who, in this sense, is his 'son' being enthroned and, by virtue of that enthronement, is ruling. At one level this applied to David and later Solomon (indeed, both Adam and Israel are referred to as 'God's son', Luke 3:38; Exod. 4:22), but only in a limited and relative way because they were finite and failed. But there was going to come a time (a 'today') when the rule would be carried out perfectly, and that day came when Jesus completed his work of saving his people by dying for them on the cross, rising from the dead and occupying heaven's throne on their behalf. That is when he 'became' God's Son in this special regal sense, such that now the Father is ruling the universe through him.

Creator of all things

Fourth, Jesus rules by virtue of *being Creator*. This has already been dealt with at length in the first four verses, but it is also here in verse 7:

> *He* makes his angels winds
>   and his ministers a flame of fire.

Who is it who 'makes' these angels? The context suggests that it is the Son.

From everlasting to everlasting

Fifth, the Son is superior by virtue of *his eternity*:

> You, Lord, laid the foundation of the earth in the
>   beginning,
>   and the heavens are the work of your hands;
> they will perish, but you remain;
>   they will all wear out like a garment,
> like a robe you will roll them up,
>   like a garment they will be changed.
> But you are the same,
>   and your years will have no end.

He is still speaking of the Son. The quotation literally begins, 'You, in the beginning, Lord',[7] so placing the person being addressed – Jesus Christ – at the same 'beginning' with which the book of Genesis commences: the creation of the heavens and the earth, including the angelic realm, for which the pre-existent Christ is also responsible. The Son existed in eternity past, he exists in eternity present and he will exist in eternity future, which is why at the end of Hebrews the writer can say, 'Jesus Christ is the same yesterday and today and for ever' (13:8). He has always been God who is able to create and save and he will always be God who is able to create and save. Little wonder that the writer goes on in chapter 2 to warn his readers not to neglect so great a salvation by drifting away from the faith. To drift away from Jesus is to drift away from God and so from salvation.

The way believers are going to keep on in the faith and be fruitful is by having this heart-pounding, awe-inspiring, worship-making view of Jesus. Reduce Jesus in any way and soon there will be little reason to remain a Christian. Christianity will then be just some kind of hobby, one amongst many. But magnify Jesus – not in the way you magnify something small by looking through a microscope, but by bringing closer to your vision something big by looking through a telescope – and then you will not only 'go' as a Christian but 'grow' as a Christian too.

It's all about Jesus

As an introduction to his 'sermon' our writer has done every-thing within his creative power to magnify Jesus. He knows

---

7 The author has changed the order of the Septuagint text (the Greek translation of the Old Testament) from 'in the beginning, you, Lord' (*kat' archas, sy kyrie*) to 'You, in the beginning, Lord' (*sy kat' archas, kyrie*).

that the Father's heart simply leaps with joy at the sight of his Son who is always before him, and the Son revels in the love of his Father who has given him all things to rule with wisdom, righteousness and power – not least a bride, the church.

Our writer wonderfully presents Christ in all his majestic glory and regal humility. As the one who is divine he brings all things into existence, and yet in his humanity he offers himself as an atoning sacrifice without for a moment relinquishing his divinity.

Jonathan Edwards tried to capture the same blend of the loftiness and lowliness of Christ:

> There do meet in Jesus Christ, infinite highness, and infinite condescension. Christ, as he is God, is infinitely great and high above all. He is higher than the kings of the earth; for he is King of Kings, and Lord of Lords. He is higher than the heavens, and higher than the highest angel of heaven … And yet he is one of infinite condescension. None are so low, or inferior, but Christ's condescension is sufficient to take gracious notice of them. He condescends not only to the angels, humbling himself to behold the things that are done in heaven, but he also condescends to such poor creatures of men … he that is thus high, condescends to take gracious notice of little children. Matthew 19:14, 'Suffer little children to come unto me.' Yes, which is much more, his condescension is sufficient to take a gracious notice of the most unworthy, sinful creatures, those who have no good deservings, and those that have infinite ill deservings.[8]

---

8 Cited in Owen Strachan and Doug Sweeney, *Jonathan Edwards on Beauty*, The Essential Edwards Collection (Chicago: Moody, 2010), pp. 84–85.

The first chapter of Hebrews uses sublime language and deep theology to draw us in to see that life, the universe and everything is all about Jesus. Everything is to be related to him. When we feel the warmth of the sun we are to praise the Son who is the Sun of righteousness with healing power in his wings. When we feel the tender rain, we are to think of the gospel showers of blessing Jesus pours out on us day by day. When we walk by a riverside our minds are to go to that stream which makes the eternal city glad and washes away our sin. In everything we are to see Jesus 'who was made lower than the angels for a little while, now crowned with glory and honour because he suffered death' (2:9).

Questions for reflection and discussion

- In the light of the argument of the writer to the Hebrews, what do you make of the statement: 'To worship Jesus if he is not God is idolatry, and to worship God without Jesus is equally idolatrous'?
- What assurances can we draw from the fact that God now rules the world as a man without ceasing to be God?
- If Jesus is God as he truly is and man as he is meant to be, how might Jesus provide a model for us to live out the full human life in him?

Prayer

O thou who in almighty power wast weak,
And in perfect excellency wast lowly, grant unto us the same mind.
All that we have which is our own is naught;
If we have any good in us it is wholly thy gift.
O Saviour, since thou, the Lord of heaven and earth,

Didst humble thyself, grant unto us true humility,
And make us like thyself;
And then, of thine infinite goodness,
Raise us to thine everlasting glory;
Who livest and reigneth with the Father and the Holy Ghost
For ever and ever.
Amen.
(Archbishop Thomas Cranmer)

Part 2

'HAIL, THE INCARNATE DEITY': A THEOLOGICAL EXPLORATION

6

Maps, models and muddles: the importance of doctrine and the incarnation

In a series of radio talks delivered during the Second World War to be later published under the title *Mere Christianity*, C. S. Lewis made an uncompromising assertion:

> Theology is practical: especially now. In the old days, when there was less education and discussion, perhaps it was possible to get on with a few simple ideas about God. But it is not so now. Everyone reads, everyone hears things discussed. Consequently, if you do not listen to Theology, that will not mean that you have no ideas about God. It will mean that you have a lot of wrong ones – bad, muddled, out-of-date ideas.[1]

Lewis was both right and wrong.

He was quite right in saying that if we give ourselves over to thinking about God we do not dispense with theology; rather, we simply take up bad theology – that is, wrong thinking which is either undisciplined and fanciful or the parroting of whatever are the fashionable ideas being trotted out by the latest out-of-date bishop. The answer to bad theology is, of course, good

---

1   C. S. Lewis, *Mere Christianity* (London: HarperCollins, 2001), p. 155.

theology: biblical, thought through, tried and tested. There is inevitability about doctrine. Doctrine at its simplest is something taught. To believe what is taught is to believe doctrine. What is crucial is ensuring that what is taught (and so believed) is true.[2]

Lewis was wrong, however, in speaking about 'the old days' when there was 'less education and discussion', such that it was possible to 'get on' with 'a few simple ideas' of God. I guess it depends which 'old days' he particularly had in mind. One of the most influential theologians in the early church was Gregory of Nyssa. Writing in the fourth century, he bemoaned the fact that it was not possible even to go shopping in the centre of Constantinople without having to put up with all sorts of theological speculation from all sorts of people:

> Constantinople is full of mechanics and slaves, every one of them profound theologians, who preach in the shops and streets. If you want someone to change a piece of silver, he tells you how the Son differs from the Father; if you ask the price for a loaf of bread, you are told that the Son is inferior to the Father; if you ask whether the bath is ready, you are told that the Son was created from nothing.[3]

Even way back then, before there were any social networks to 'get out there' into the wider public world whatever was 'in here' in their private thought worlds, people were having a good old time sounding off on their own views about the incarnation. It follows that there needs to be some way of sifting

---

2 'Even those who believe in nothing hold to a doctrine (nihilism). Doctrine is here to stay. The only question is whether it is Christian or non-Christian, healthy or toxic.' Kevin J. Vanhoozer, *Pictures at a Theological Exhibition* (London: Inter-Varsity Press, 2016), p. 52.

3 Cited by Alister McGrath, *Studies in Doctrine* (Grand Rapids: Zondervan, 1997), p. 23.

the grain of God-given truth from the chaff of wasteful speculation.

This is where doctrine comes in.

There are basically two ways we can think about doctrine and the role it plays in the church and the life of the Christian. The first is that of a map.

Maps are very useful if you not only want to get from A to B in good time without getting lost, but you also want to enjoy the journey, noting interesting sites along the way. Christian doctrines about God, the Trinity, the person of Christ, humankind, heaven and hell, and so on, act like that. They are practical in that they help us think about God properly and so enjoy him more deeply.

For example, is there anything more practical and important for the Christian than worship? Probably one of the best definitions of worship was that given by Archbishop William Temple:

> Worship is the submission of all our nature to God. It is the quickening of conscience by his holiness; the nourishment of mind with his truth; the purifying of imagination by his beauty; the opening of the heart to his love; the surrender of will to his purpose – and all this gathered up in adoration, the most selfless emotion of which our nature is capable and therefore the chief remedy for the self-centredness which is our original sin and the source of all actual sin.[4]

How can our consciences be quickened by God's holiness unless we know what holiness *is*? How is it possible to have our

---

4 William Temple, *Readings in St John's Gospel* (London: Macmillan, 1940), p. 68.

minds nourished unless we know what the truth is? Our imaginations will remain dull and unenlightened unless we are given a glimpse of the beauty of God, which involves contemplating the divine attributes – the great 'omni's: omnipotence, omniscience, omnipresence. Doctrine is crucial for proper worship. It is a false choice to be confronted with either devotion or doctrine, for without true doctrine there will never be true devotion: 'Theology without worship is empty; worship without theology is blind.'[5]

It is also important to point out that there are different *types* of maps designed to achieve different purposes. Not only are there road maps which are primarily drawn up to enable travel, but there are geological maps to help ascertain the underlying structure of an area; topographical maps to delineate the terrain; meteorological maps to help predict the weather, and so on. It is similar in theology. Some of the 'maps' which theologians have drawn up are more like travel maps helping us to orientate ourselves on our Christian journey in relation to God, the world and the world to come. Others take us deeper into the 'substructure' – the being and nature of God; for example, how Jesus is one person and yet comprises two natures, being fully divine and fully human.

The second way of thinking about doctrine is that of a model.[6] Models have been very useful in the development of science. Think, for example, of the model proposed by James Watson

---

5 McGrath, *Studies in Doctrine*, p. 117.
6 A model is a theoretical construct which is recognized as analogical and acts as an aid to understand data or experience. This is the way Ian Barbour describes models: 'Models and theories are imaginative human constructs. Models, on this reading, are to be taken seriously but not literally; they are neither literal pictures nor useful fictions but limited and inadequate ways of imagining what is not observable. They make tentative ontological claims that there are entities in the world something like those postulated in the models.' Ian G. Barbour, *Religion and Science: Historical and Contemporary Issues* (London: Harper Collins, 1997), pp. 115–124.

and Francis Crick of the 'double helix' molecule of which our hereditary material is composed – the basic unit of life. It is not being suggested that if it were possible to 'blow up' a molecule so that it became visible to the naked eye, this is *exactly* what we would see; rather, models provide scientists with ways of getting to grips with natural phenomena, of conceptualizing things. This doesn't mean that the models are 'make-believe' and have no correspondence to what they seek to depict; on the contrary, some models have a high degree of correspondence. Likewise, the Bible provides 'verbal pictures' or 'models' of God using a whole variety of images which together form God's self-disclosure: that God is Father, Son and Holy Spirit, a shepherd, king, husband. Some of these models take us very close to the heart of God's character and how he chooses to relate to us, while others are of a lower order of significance but play a part nonetheless in God's overall self-revelation.

In theology, models are used to represent the 'reality in Christ'. They have both a positive and a negative role. Positively, they help set forth the truth as God has revealed it in the Bible, thus giving us appropriate ways of thinking about him. Negatively, they set limits, marking off the boundaries beyond which certain ideas should *not* be entertained because they are both misleading and dangerous in that they lead to idolatry – 'vain' or 'empty' thoughts of God. Although they may draw on traditional theological language, they do not constitute theology 'proper'. For example, to speak of God as 'mother' instead of 'father' leads to a wholly different conception of God from that which is given to us in Scripture.[7]

---

7 See Melvin Tinker, 'Is God Female?', in *Touchy Topics* (Evangelical Press: Welwyn Garden City, 2016), pp. 47–63.

The early church went to great lengths to ensure that the 'models' which were to be drawn up to help us think of God, and so worship him aright, were faithful to the Bible's own testimony. This meant guarding against misunderstandings as well as encouraging careful, and sometimes delicately nuanced, thinking about God. This led to the formulation of what have become known as the great Catholic Creeds, that is, creedal statements about Christian beliefs (*credo*, 'I believe') which the whole church accepted as valid (in this sense being 'catholic' or 'universal').

In the chapters that follow we shall be looking in a little more detail at some of these creeds and especially at the wrong beliefs (heresies) which they were designed to counter and correct. This will hopefully help us clarify our own thinking about the incarnation: what it means and why it matters.

As a kind of preliminary to those two questions, Fred Sanders raises a related question, namely, is the incarnation – that God should become man, as Christians celebrate each Christmas – *appropriate*? Here are the reasons why he thinks it is *wholly* appropriate for God to do such a thing:

> First, because it's appropriate for God to make himself known to creatures through creaturely means. 'The invisible things of God' are always being made known through visible, created things. The incarnation, rather than contradicting that principle, is the ultimate instantiation of it.
>
> Second, because God's very nature is goodness, a goodness which communicates itself to others. So from God's side of things, it is perfectly appropriate, and eminently

fitting, to make himself known and present to human creatures.

There are other reasons, drawn from God himself, that the incarnation is rightly understood as appropriate. Considering these in the right way, we can glimpse why it is not unbecoming for God to become human.

But there, in the pun on 'unbecoming' and 'becoming', we need to surface one more faulty presupposition for examination. Because the Bible says that God became man, or 'the word became flesh', we sometimes allow ourselves to think that in this event God stopped being what he was, and morphed instead into what he had not previously been. That's not what the Bible means here, and it's not what incarnation is. Instead, without ceasing to be fully divine, God the Son added to himself human nature. God did not change; it would be better to say that human nature changed in relation to God by being brought into this new relation to the immutable God. Understanding it this way (as you have to, unless you're ready to redefine 'God' sub-biblically as 'one of those changing things') requires a kind of Copernican revolution of the theological mind: we thought we were describing how God's nature arced across our sky and revolved around us, but had to admit that God's nature arcs across our sky precisely because we revolve around him.[8]

Hopefully, this book will help us to engage in that theological Copernican revolution.

---

8 Fred Sanders, 'Incarnation: How Appropriate', The Scriptorium Daily, 26 December 2017, <http://scriptoriumdaily.com/incarnation-how-appropriate/2017>.

But just in case there is still the sneaking suspicion that talk of 'doctrine' and 'dogma' makes for boredom rather than worship, these words of someone whose mind was steeped in drama and creativity should act as a check:

> So that is the outline of the official story – the tale of the time when God was the underdog and got beaten, when he submitted to the conditions he had laid down and became a man like the men he had made, and the men he had made broke him and killed him. This is the dogma we find so dull – this terrifying drama of which God is the victim and hero . . . If this is dull, what, in heaven's name, is worthy to be called exciting?!

Working up to her conclusion Dorothy L. Sayers drives home the point even further:

> Now, we may call that doctrine exhilarating, or we may call it devastating; we may call it revelation, or we may call it rubbish; but if we call it dull, then words have no meaning at all. That God should play the tyrant over man is the usual dreary record of human futility; but that man should play the tyrant over God and find him a better man than himself is an astonishing drama indeed. Any journalist, hearing of it for the first time, would recognise it as news; those who did hear it for the first time actually called it news, and good news at that; though we are likely to forget that the word *Gospel* ever meant anything but sensational.[9]

---

9   Dorothy L. Sayers, 'The Greatest Drama Ever Staged', in *The Whimsical Christian: 18 Essays of Dorothy Sayers* (Boston: Hall, 1979), pp. 24–25.

And so we turn to the sensational news of the time when God became a man and ask: what do we mean when we speak of 'incarnation'?

7

'He came down to earth from heaven'

The 'incarnation' of Christ literally means his 'en-fleshment' (Greek *ensarkosis*) or, as the early Fathers sometimes put it, the 'en-manning of the eternal Son of God'. It is the doctrine expressed in the opening pages of John's Gospel which reaches its climax in 1:14: 'The Word became flesh and dwelt among us.' This is a pretty good place to begin in our thinking.

The one who became incarnate was the Word (Logos). The incarnation presupposes both the prior existence of Christ and his divine status. His existence didn't begin with his birth from the Virgin: he 'was from the beginning'. In the beginning he was God: 'In the beginning was the Word, and the Word was with God, and the Word *was* God' (John 1:1). Therefore, before the Word became flesh in time (*logos ensarkos*) he was without flesh in eternity (*logos asarkos*).

What John also makes clear is that of the three persons of the Godhead, the one who became incarnate was specifically the second person: God the Word, or God the Son: 'And the *Word became flesh* and dwelt among us, and we have seen his glory, glory as of the only Son from the Father, full of grace and truth' (John 1:14). The Father did not become incarnate. Neither did the Holy Spirit. It was the second person alone who underwent this 'transformative' experience, if we may put it like that. And so we need to be a little careful in our prayers if we find ourselves praying, 'Father, thank you for dying for us on the cross.' He didn't – that was the Son!

Note, too, that John speaks of Christ as *becoming* 'flesh' (v. 14). This is in deliberate contrast to his earlier statement, 'the Word was God'. We are never told that he *became* God.

There is a change of tense, as well as a change of verb. The imperfect tense used in verse 1 tells us of the eternal being of God the Son: he always was and always will be God. But the verb 'became' in verse 14 is not imperfect, it is in the aorist or punctiliar tense. The Word was not always flesh; he became flesh at one *particular*, decisive *moment* in history.

That he became flesh means he became man.

What 'became' means . . . and doesn't mean

What Christians celebrate at Christmas is nothing less than God becoming a man, taking on a genuine human nature. This means that it was more than his inhabiting a human body (which is where the term 'en-fleshment' can be rather misleading); he became whatever it took to be human – 'mind, body and soul', to use the tripartite division – while (and this is important) *remaining God* in an undiminished way. Jesus was fully God *and* fully man. This was not a matter of a man 'being raised up' into God, but of God 'coming down' to become a man: 'He came down to earth from heaven / who is God and Lord of all' (in the words of Cecil Frances Alexander in 'Once in Royal David's City'). The person of the eternal Son comes down to us, takes on human nature without relinquishing or compromising his divine nature, and therefore remains God in doing so.

This is what Christians call a 'mystery', something which goes beyond anything a human mind could possibly fathom ('Great indeed . . . is the mystery of godliness', 1 Tim. 3:16). We therefore have to be very careful when we try to reach for analogies or illustrations to convey that mystery.

For example, here is C. S. Lewis:

> The Second Person in God, the Son, became human himself: was born into the world as an actual man – a real man of a particular height, with hair of a particular colour, speaking in a particular language, weighing so many stone. The Eternal Being, who knows everything and who created the whole universe, became not only a man but (before that) a baby, and before that a foetus inside a Woman's body. If you want to get the hang of it, think how you would like to become a slug or a crab.[1]

Of course, what Lewis says in the first part of this statement is fully in line with what we have seen so far: the second person of the Trinity becoming a specific and entire human being, Jesus of Nazareth. But by going on to say that if we want to 'get the hang of it', we should imagine what it would be like for us to become 'a slug or a crab', Lewis starts to unravel the doctrine because for us this would mean becoming something *wholly other* than what we are, while the Son *continued to remain* what he was – God – retaining the divine nature while becoming man. As we shall see in a later chapter, there is something about the way God has made humans which in principle makes the incarnation a possibility.

---

1 C. S. Lewis, *Mere Christianity* (London: HarperCollins, 2001), p. 179.

Paul Helm draws attention to what might be considered the faintest analogy to what happened when God became man without ceasing to be God.[2] He argues that God did not become man in the sense in which a table becomes ashes, but much more like when a man and a woman become a husband and a wife in marriage. They remain a man and a woman, but in marrying they enter into a new relationship. Similarly, but in a unique and unparalleled way, God the Son remains God the Son while entering into a new relationship, united to human nature in the person of Jesus of Nazareth. But even this has to be heavily qualified as in marriage there is a union of two persons who share the same nature – humanity (a person is the 'who' and the nature the 'what') – but with the incarnation there is a union of two *natures* (divine and human) in *one* person, whilst ensuring that the natures remain distinct! Now you can see why Christians speak of the *mystery* of the incarnation! It is unique, without any earthly parallel. It is *sui generis*.

Condescension without being 'condescending'

There is always a fine balancing act to be maintained when thinking of the incarnation. If we lean too far in either direction we fall off the theological high wire into heresy (and, as we shall see, church history is replete with examples). Go too far in one direction in wanting to secure Jesus' divine nature and we end up diminishing his human nature: he simply 'appears' to be

---

2 Paul Helm, 'Incomprehensibly Made Man', Helm's Deep (blog), 1 December 2008, <https://paulhelmsdeep.blogspot.com/search?q=%E2%80%98Incomprehensibly+made+man%E2%80%99>.

human, with the human body of Jesus acting like a kind of space suit in which the divine being can survive for a while in a hostile environment ('God in a pod'). Go too far in the other direction in stressing his humanity and his deity is compromised: Jesus is merely *like* God but is *not really* God. Being true to the biblical data means we must affirm that in the incarnation God was not in any way diminished, with God lessening himself in order to 'shrink' into human nature. Throughout it all, God remained wholly and completely *God*. This has some glorious implications concerning the divine activities – if we can call them that – of the Son while on earth, so much so that we shall devote a whole chapter to the subject (chapter 10). At this point, let it suffice to emphasize that the one person (the Son) possessed two natures in the incarnation, divinity and humanity, without diminishing or compromising either.

Perhaps the term which most faithfully captures this downward movement of the second person of the Trinity is 'condescension'. Today when we speak of someone acting in a condescending manner, we mean that they 'stoop down' reluctantly, acting 'beneath themselves'. It is more or less equivalent to being 'patronizing'. The biblical idea captured by this word, however, is altogether different and quite breathtakingly wonderful.

A hymn to humility

There is a 'hymn' in the Bible which captures the thought beautifully: it is Philippians 2:6–11, especially verse 5:

Who, being in the form of God, did not consider equality with God something to be grasped, but emptied himself,

'He came down to earth from heaven'

taking the form of a slave, in the likeness of men, being found in the form of a man, he humbled himself becoming obedient to death.
(My translation)

Christ's status is asserted as nothing less than divine: 'the form of God'. He was equal in divinity with God the Father. All that belongs to the 'godness' of God also belongs to the one called 'the Son'. Such words as omniscience, omnipotence and omnipresence rightly apply to him, for he is the all-knowing, all-powerful, all-present deity.

We are then astonished at what he does with this privileged position – or rather, what he *doesn't* do. He doesn't exploit it to his own advantage; instead, he displays what true divinity is, namely, 'self-giving'. Whilst literally having the divine right to wholly remain in heaven, to hold onto his power and prestige, if you will, he exercises a different divine right: the right to be humble and to change his 'form' whilst not ceasing to be God. We are told in the song that he 'emptied' (*ekenōsen*) himself. This does not mean that he emptied himself *of* something, otherwise he would have lost his 'godness'; rather, he emptied himself in the sense that he *took on* something: human nature, the 'form' of a man and the 'form' of a slave. His divine form was hidden under the veil of his human form.[3] Occasionally

---

3 Richard Bauckham argues that this passage does not suggest any diminishing of Christ's divinity: in 'the phrase *to einai isa theō* ("being equal with God", "equality with God") . . . there is no question here of either gaining or losing equality with God. The pre-existent Christ has equality with God; the issue is his attitude to it. He elects to express it, not by continuing to enjoy "the form of God" (*morphē theou*), which is the visible splendour of the divine status of heaven, but by exchanging this glorious form for the humble status of the human form (*morphēn doulou*) on earth.' Richard Bauckham, *Jesus and the God of Israel: God Crucified and Other Studies on the New Testament's Christology of Divine Identity* (Carlisle: Paternoster Press, 2008), pp. 206–207. Or as Bruce Milne writes, 'At a theological level kenosis [the idea of divine

that veil was lifted; for example, on the Mount of Transfiguration (Matt. 17:1–17). There for one brief moment the 'form of God', the visible splendour of the divine status of heaven, shone with a blinding brilliance. But for most of his earthly life the veil remained firmly in place. In the words of the Danish philosopher Søren Kierkegaard, Jesus was 'the divine incognito'; or in the words of Charles Wesley, 'Veiled in flesh the Godhead see / Hail, the incarnate deity.'

As the Swiss theologian Karl Barth put it, in the incarnation there is an unveiling *in* the veiling. God veils himself in humanity, being truly human, but in so doing he unveils to us what true deity is like. It enabled people to 'see the glory' of God's 'one and only', and that glory – the heart of 'godness' – is 'grace and truth' (John 1:14).

> Jesus Christ is what you get when God condescends to us in this way. Veiled, but not blotted out, not wholly hidden . . . paradoxically the veiling is also a revealing of God. For it tells us what God is when his glory is 'refracted' by being in union with human nature. Just as a light bulb is one way of showing us what electricity is like, and an electric shock is another way, so the Incarnation is the God-ordained way of showing us what God is like.[4]

The nineteenth-century Princeton theologian B. B. Warfield commented as follows on the *ekenōsen* verb which lies at the heart of the condescension of the incarnation:

(note 3 *cont.*) self-emptying] appears to move in the wrong direction. Its basic equation is: incarnation = God minus. The biblical equation is rather: incarnation = God plus.'
Bruce Milne, *Know the Truth: A Handbook of Christian Belief* (Leicester: Inter-Varsity Press, 2009), p. 200.
4   Helm, 'Incomprehensibly Made Man'.

Paul, in a word, says here nothing more than that our Lord, who did not look with greedy eyes upon His state of equality with God, emptied Himself, if the language may be pardoned, of Himself; that is to say, in precise accordance with the exhortation for the enhancement of which His example is adduced, that He did not look on His own things ... He took the 'form of a servant', and so was 'made in the likeness of men'. But His doing this showed that He did not set overweening store by His state of equality with God, and did not count Himself the sufficient object of all the efforts. He was not self-regarding: He had regard for others. Thus He becomes our supreme example of self-abnegating conduct.[5]

Again, we must be careful not to misunderstand what we are reading here. It is not that the Son did something *contrary* to his divine nature: being humble and other-person-centred which he was 'forced' to do out of necessity to achieve our salvation. Rather, the self-abnegation *is* a revelation of the divine nature; this is what God is *like* within his own being. We worship a humble God, one who is exalted in his lowliness and regal in his service.

Furthermore, as Paul goes on to show by speaking about Jesus' humbling himself to death, even 'death on a cross', it is through a kind of 'passivity' that Jesus brings about our redemption, so the *mode* of the incarnation is integrally linked to the *means* of salvation:

---

5   B. B. Warfield, *The Person and Work of Christ* (ed. Samuel G. Craig; Philadelphia: Presbyterian & Reformed, 1950), pp. 42–43. For a helpful discussion on Warfield's insight into the incarnation as expressed in Phil. 2, see Carl R. Trueman, 'The Glory of Christ: B. B. Warfield on Jesus of Nazareth', in *The Wages of Spin* (Fearn, Ross-shire: Mentor, 2004), pp. 103–128.

When we look closer at that language, we see that Christ's conquering is achieved through a kind of passivity, through suffering, through renunciation and dedication to the will of his Father. When tempted into physical combat he resists, he scorns weapons, and rebukes his follower Peter, commanding him to put his sword away. He could have called legions of angels to defeat the forces. He won a victory, to be sure, and he triumphantly led a host to the enjoyment of it, but this is a victory in which ends and means were perfectly suited, in which the victory was secured by a resistance to temptation and sin that was total.[6]

God comes down to lift man up

Whilst it has been emphasized that the incarnation is the great act of condescension by God and not the elevation of a mere man (the heresy of adoptionism), nonetheless it does entail an elevation of man, in two senses.

First, in his assuming human nature, true humanity has been taken into God, and it is as a *man* that Christ now reigns in heaven. Karl Barth expressed this eloquently when he wrote,

He is the Lord humbled for communion with man and likewise the Servant exalted to communion with God. He is the Word spoken from the loftiest, most luminous transcendence and likewise the Word heard in the deepest, darkest immanence. He is both, without their

---

6 Paul Helm, 'Two Approaches to the Incarnation', Helm's Deep (blog), 26 March 2010, <https://paulhelmsdeep.blogspot.com/search?q=Incarnation+as+Condescension %E2%80%99>.

being confused but also without their being divided; He is wholly the one and wholly the other. Thus in this oneness Jesus Christ is the Mediator, the Reconciler, between God and man.[7]

Second, the incarnation is the *visible beginning* of God's mighty acts of redemption in his Son. By virtue of his coming, dying, rising from the dead and glorious ascension, there is through our union *with* him our exaltation *in* him. The technical term for this is *theopoiesis*, whereby the Son of God became what we are (yet without sin) so that we might become what he is (participating in the 'divine nature', 2 Pet. 1:4). Here are just a few citations from theologians throughout the centuries which, in different ways, convey the same idea:[8]

- Irenaeus in the second century writes of 'The Word of God, our Lord Jesus Christ, who did, through His transcendent love, become what we are, that He might bring us to be even what he is in himself' (*Against Heresies* 5, preface).
- The fourth-century theologian Athanasius writes that Jesus 'prayed for us, taking on Him what is ours, and He was giving what He received ... For as He for our sake became man, so we for His sake are exalted' (*Against the Arians* 4.7).
- Also in the fourth century we find Gregory of Nazianzus stating, 'He came down that we might be exalted ... He ascended that He might draw to Himself us, who were lying low in the Fall of sin' (*Oration* 1, 5).

---

7 Karl Barth, *The Humanity of God* (Louisville: John Knox Press, 1960), p. 46.
8 Cited in Gerrit Scott Dawson, *Jesus Ascended: The Meaning of Christ's Continuing Incarnation* (Edinburgh: T&T Clark, 2004), pp. 164–165.

- Leo the Great in the fifth century declares that Jesus in his union with us is declaring, 'For I have united you to Myself, and am become the Son of Man that you might have power to be sons of God' (*Sermons* 5).
- Moving on to the sixteenth century, Calvin, following Athanasius at this point, writes, 'This is the wonderful exchange which, out of his measureless benevolence, Jesus Christ has made with us; that, becoming Son of man with us, he has made us sons of God with him; that, by his descent into death, he has prepared an ascent into heaven for us' (*Institutes* 4:17.2).
- Finally, we have Andrew Murray in the late nineteenth century in his exposition of Hebrews stating 'that the knowledge of Jesus as having entered heaven for us, and taken us in union with Himself into a heavenly life, is what will deliver the Christian from all that is low and feeble, and lift him into a life of joy and strength. To gaze upon the beauty of the heavenly Christ in the Father's presence, to whom all things are subject, will transform us into heavenly Christians, dwelling all the day in God's presence and overcoming every enemy' (*Holiest of All*).

It would be more accurate (and less misleading) to think of our exaltation in Christ which is attendant upon his humiliation as not so much *deification* but as our true *humanization*. Athanasius, the great defender of orthodoxy, was careful to draw the boundaries at this point:

And He said this too, not that we might become such as the Father; for to become as the Father, is impossible for us creatures, who have been brought out of nothing . . .

For as, although there be one Son by nature, True and Only-begotten, we too become sons, not as He in nature and truth, but according to the grace of Him that calleth, and though we are men from the earth, are yet called gods, not as the True God or His Word, but as He has pleased God who has given that grace.
(*Against the Arians* 3.25.19)

It is by our union with Christ by the Holy Spirit who is also at work in us that we become 'sons of God'. Athanasius continues,

by the participation of the Spirit we are knit into the Godhead; so that our being in the Father is not ours, but is the Spirit's which is in us and abides in us . . . For what the Word has by nature, as I said in the Father, that He wishes to be given to us through the Spirit irrevocably.
(*Against the Arians* 3.25.24–25)[9]

Athanasius has in mind the words of Jesus when he said, 'In that day you will know that I am in my Father, and you in me, and I in you' (John 14:20) and '. . . may all be one, just as you, Father, are in me, and I in you, that they also may be in us' (John 17:21).

All of this discussion underscores the fact that key doctrines such as incarnation, redemption, resurrection, ascension and glorification are inextricably linked in the great theological matrix of salvation.

T. F. Torrance warns against developing a kind of spiritual vertigo when we contemplate the depths to which Christ

---

9 Cited in Dawson, *Jesus Ascended*, p. 167.

descended and the lofty heights to which we now ascend in him: 'Through the Spirit Christ is nearer to us than we are to ourselves, and we who live and dwell on earth are yet made to sit with Christ "in the heavenly places", partaking of the divine nature in him.'[10]

Incomprehensibly made man

Sometimes theology is better expressed by poetry than prose. We end this section with both in order to summarize the theme that we have been developing: that God became man without ceasing to be God.

First, Charles Wesley:

> Let earth and heaven combine,
> Angels and men agree,
> To praise in songs divine
> The incarnate Deity,
> Our God contracted to a span,
> Incomprehensibly made man.

Second, Augustine of Hippo at his most poetic:

> Wherefore the Word of God, who is also the Son of God, co-eternal with the Father, the Power and the Wisdom of God, mightily pervading and harmoniously ordering all things, from the highest limit of the intelligent to the lowest limit of the material creation, revealed and concealed, nowhere confined, nowhere divided, nowhere distended, but without dimensions, everywhere present

---

10 T. F. Torrance, *Space, Time and Resurrection* (Edinburgh: T&T Clark, 1969), p. 135.

in His entirety, – this Word of God, I say, took to Himself, in a manner entirely different from that in which He is present to other creatures, the soul and body of a man, and made, by the union of Himself therewith, the one person Jesus Christ. Mediator between God and men, in His Deity equal with the Father, in His flesh, i.e. in His human nature, inferior to the Father, – unchangeably immortal in respect of the divine nature, in which He is equal with the Father, and yet changeable and mortal in respect of the infirmity which was His through participation with our nature.

(*Letter to Volusian*, 137)[11]

The Creator becomes a creature, the Sovereign takes on the role of a servant, and the worshipped One becomes the rejected One. This is incarnation.

Whoever said that theology was dull?!

Questions for reflection and discussion

- Why is it important to hold to the notion of 'mystery' when speaking of the incarnation? How would you counter the suggestion that Christians speak of 'mystery' because they are entertaining a nonsense idea and it provides a convenient curtain to hide behind?
- How does the idea of Christ's 'self-emptying' in the incarnation give us insight into the character of God?
- How might the 'wonderful exchange' fuel our devotion to Christ?

---

11 Cited by Helm, 'Incomprehensibly Made Man'.

Prayer

Almighty God, give us grace that we may cast away the works of darkness, and put upon us the armour of light, now in the time of this mortal life, in which thy Son Jesus Christ came to visit us in great humility; that in the last day, when he shall come again in his glorious Majesty to judge both the quick and the dead, we may rise to the life immortal, through him who liveth and reigneth with thee and the Holy Spirit, now and for ever. Amen.

(Book of Common Prayer, Collect for the First Sunday in Advent)

8

Creeds avoiding chaos

When I studied theology at Oxford University, one of my tutors in early church history was a Jesuit priest who resided at a college called Campion Hall. As I climbed the stairway leading to his room each Wednesday afternoon for my tutorial during Hilary term, I had to pass a large painting of a man dressed in full bishop's regalia with a small boy on the beach by the sea. The painting portrayed a story which went something like this: Once, the great fourth-century theologian Bishop Augustine of Hippo was doing some work on the Trinity. As he walked along the beach one day in order to clear his mind, he came across a boy pouring sea water into a hole he had dug in the sand. Augustine watched the lad for some time and then asked: 'What are you doing?'

'Why,' said the boy, 'I am pouring the Mediterranean sea into my hole.'

'Don't be silly,' said Augustine, 'you can't fit the sea into that little hole. You are wasting your time.'

To which the little boy retorted, 'Well, so are you wasting *your* time trying to write a book about God!'

This apocryphal story makes a telling point, namely, that as mere humans we can never get God completely taped any more than a little boy can get the whole Mediterranean Sea into a hole on the beach. However, that doesn't mean it is not worthwhile attempting some measure of understanding of God; after all, it could be argued that the boy did manage to get *some* of the Mediterranean into his hole! Likewise, we might at least expect to know something of God if not everything about him, especially since it is God who has taken the initiative to make himself known by special revelation, as we saw in chapter 1: God spoke in bits and pieces in the past through the prophets, and now he speaks fully in his Son. To attempt to speak truly of God is precisely what some of the early Church Fathers tried to do, with varying degrees of success.

Which matters matter

Fred Sanders rightly argues that

> Though the body of Christian truth is made up of a great many doctrines, perhaps hundreds of them, there are only three great mysteries at the very heart of Christianity: the atonement, the incarnation, and the Trinity. All the lesser doctrines depend upon these great truths, derive their significance from them, and spell out their implications.[1]

In order to see off heretical views and establish beliefs which arose out of, and were in line with, the Bible, various church leaders met in what were called 'ecumenical councils' at which were forged statements of belief called creeds which primarily addressed two of those 'three great mysteries': the incarnation and the Trinity. The first three councils and the creeds formulated there (held at Nicaea, Constantinople and Ephesus respectively) found their climax in Chalcedon held in AD 451.

---

1 Fred Sanders, 'Chalcedonian Categories for the Gospel Narrative', in Fred Sanders and Klaus Issler (eds.), *Jesus in Trinitarian Perspective: An Introductory Christology* (Nashville: Broadman & Holman, 2007), pp. 1–43 [8].

This was the *key* council which helped consolidate thinking on the person of Christ.

What the 'Chalcedonian Definition' provided was the framework within which the identity of Jesus could be properly discussed. It helped furnish the church with the fundamental categories to operate with, making it clear which were the main *wrong* ways of thinking about Christ; and it drew up some of the boundaries which were not to be crossed conceptually, whilst at the same time providing the proper 'field of play' within which the correct answers were to be located.

There were basically four boundaries drawn for thinking about the person and nature of Jesus Christ.

The first is that Jesus is *fully God*. Not part God, not like God, but truly and fully God – true deity.

The second boundary condition is that Jesus is *fully human*. All that makes for a human being, Jesus was and is – true humanity.

The third boundary is that Jesus has *two natures*, a divine nature and a human nature; this logically follows from the first two propositions.

The fourth is that Jesus is *one person* (the technical term is *hypostasis*).

Boundaries of freedom

Some scholars give the impression that it is rather restrictive to speak of 'boundaries' in this way. They argue that it hampers creative and exploratory thought. But this is a strange objection. As I write, the FIFA World Cup is in full swing and millions of people throughout the world are glued to their TV screens or tuned to their radios to enjoy some of the best players on the planet displaying their soccer prowess with relish. Think of what would happen if some of the players decided to change not only the rules of the game but also the way in which the game is played on the basis of the objection that the present rules 'restrict their creativity'. Supposing some players decided to use two balls instead of one, or to dribble the ball outside the boundaries of the field and still claim that the goal they scored was valid! Here the game of soccer would not be enriched (no matter how much the players claimed it enhanced their performance), it would be destroyed. Rules and boundaries are necessary not only for any sporting endeavour, but also for any intellectual endeavour. This is especially so when we are dealing with what are claimed to be divine truths. Nothing less than the eternal salvation of people and the well-being of the church is at stake.

Each ecumenical council produced formulations to help the church understand the identity of Jesus and which effectively countered a prevailing wrong view which was doing the rounds at the time.

Jesus is God: Nicaea, AD 325

Arius was a teacher in the church of Alexandria in the fourth century and in many ways can be thought of as the distant ancestor of the Jehovah's Witnesses, for he taught that Jesus was not eternally the Son of God. His famous statement about Christ, which created such a furore, ran: 'There was a time when the Son was not.' For Arius, Jesus was a creature – not an ordinary creature, to be sure, but a kind of 'super-creature', not quite human, not God, but the highest kind of creature through whom God related to the world.

Arius employed simple (simplistic?) reasoning which ran along the lines of a syllogism involving a major premise, a minor premise and a conclusion:

Major premise: If Jesus is the *Son* of God he must have been begotten.
Minor premise: If he was begotten there must have been a time *before* he was begotten.
Conclusion: Jesus is not eternal (as God is) but a *creature* God brought into being (begotten) and through whom the world was made.

Hence the Arian rallying cry, 'There was a time when the Son was not.'

How can we be saved?

Here is one of those instances which highlight how doctrines are interconnected.

We saw as we looked at the first chapter of Hebrews that it was a 'given' for the Jews that *only* God – the LORD – could save (e.g. Isa. 46:13). But according to Arius Jesus was not God, so how could he save? To use the theological jargon, Christology (who Jesus is) is linked to soteriology (what Jesus came to do: bring salvation).

Furthermore, Jesus was not fully human either. This would mean that Jesus was not able to fulfil the role of a human mediator, representing humanity to God as a man, which, according to the writer to the Hebrews, is a requirement for a faithful high priest (Heb. 2:14; 4:15).

It was at this level of having an inadequate view of salvation that Arius was challenged by the church leader Athanasius. He followed a *biblical* logic. Only God can save, so Jesus must be

God to fulfil this necessary condition, or he is no Saviour at all. If God has been personally offended by man, then God must personally forgive those offences against *him*; this can't be delegated to someone else, God himself must do it. Furthermore, since it is man who has done the offending there needs to be a man who will represent man. The upshot is the need for someone who is both God *and* man; and the biblical testimony is that Jesus Christ meets both requirements.

Maurice Wiles helpfully summarizes Athanasius's position over and against that of Arius:

> To Athanasius, Arianism was not a misleading interpretation of Christianity; it was not Christianity at all. It could be Judaism with its solitary God; it could be Greek philosophy with its 'unbegotten' replacing the Father God of the Bible; it could be Greek polytheism with its gods of different rank. The one thing it could not be was Christianity ... Only a truly divine saviour could save; only one who was divine absolutely in his own right could impart to man a share of his own divine nature, could make them 'partakers of the divine nature' (2 Peter 1:4) which was the essence of salvation. Arianism spelt doom to all the religious values of Christianity; it was the death of Christian religion. No true progress could be made unless it were absolutely and unequivocally rejected.[2]

Getting things clear

In AD 325 Athanasius (as a junior minister at the time called a deacon) and a group of church leaders (bishops) gathered in the

---

2   Maurice Wiles, *The Christian Fathers* (Oxford: Oxford University Press, 1982), pp. 40–41.

town of Nicaea, now Iznik on the west coast of Turkey. Here they produced what came to be known as the 'Nicene Creed' or creed of Nicaea. The key phrase which nailed the lid of the coffin of Arius is the declaration:

> We believe . . . In one Lord Jesus Christ the Son of God, begotten as only begotten of the Father, [that is, of the substance, *ousia*, with the Father], God of God, Light of Light, true God of true God, begotten not made con-substantial [of the same substance, *homoousios*] with the Father, through whom all things came into existence, both things in heaven and things on earth; who for us and our salvation came down and was incarnate and became man, suffered and rose again the third day, ascended into the heavens, is coming to judge the living and the dead.

And just to make sure the Arians were completely skewered, an anathema or curse was attached:

> But those who say, 'There was a time when he did not exist', and 'Before being begotten he did not exist', and that he came into being from non-existence, or who allege that the Son of God is of another hypostasis or *ousia*, or who is alterable or changeable, these the Catholic and Apostolic Church condemns.

The creed positively affirms that God the Son had always existed and was eternally begotten of the Father, so there never was a time (if there is 'time' in eternity) when he did not exist, contra Arius. What is more, he was of one substance (same) with the Father – that is, he was equally God, not a different

111

substance *like* God, but truly God. He shared in the 'godness of God'. In the Greek, the difference between the two words consists of a difference in one letter, iota, 'i'. For Athanasius, Jesus was the same substance (*homoousios*) with the Father – 'one'. For the compromisers, the so-called 'Semi-Arians', Jesus was *homoiousios* with the Father, 'like substance'. But that one letter makes all the difference in the world; after all, there is only one letter difference between the words 'theist' and 'atheist'! In the creed the difference is between Jesus being Creator and him being a creature.

By the end of the fourth century, Arianism was excluded from the church – which is not the same as saying that the idea died out: it is still around today, as mentioned earlier, in the form of the beliefs of the Jehovah's Witnesses. But the belief was firmly established: Jesus Christ is fully God.

Jesus is fully human: Constantinople, AD 381

Sometimes being zealous against one error can result in inadvertently falling into an equal and opposite error. This was certainly the case with Apollinaris, a bishop from Laodicea who was a strident opponent of Arius.

Here we have an example of taking biblical terminology but pushing it in a direction which is at odds with the Bible itself. We saw that in John 1, the second person of the Godhead is referred to as the Logos or Word. The 'problem' was that it was a term which had a wide range of meanings. Not only could it mean 'word', but it could also mean 'reason' or 'rationality'.[3]

---

3   This was also linked to what some considered to be truly human; for example, Aristotle defined man as a 'rational animal' and uses for 'rational' the Greek word *logikos*.

Apollinaris held that the divine Logos replaced what would otherwise have been Christ's human 'rational soul'. To understand how this would work we need to be aware of the Platonic psychology from which it was derived.

This saw the soul being divided up into a hierarchy of three 'layers': the *appetitive* (which, as the name suggests, is concerned with basic bodily desires: food, sleep, sex, and so on); the *emotional*; and the *rational*. Apollinaris conceded that Christ had assumed the lower parts of the human soul, which would account for the biblical references to his sufferings, hunger, tiredness, and so on, but he claimed that the highest rational part was directly *replaced* by the divine Logos.

'God in a pod'

The problem with this formulation was that it compromised Jesus' humanity; he was not *fully* human, for there was one part of his humanity which had been replaced, namely, his rational soul. Jesus' body effectively became some kind of 'space suit' for an extra-terrestrial 'logos' to occupy during his sojourn on Planet Earth – a kind of 'God in a pod'. This was more or less admitted by Apollinaris himself: 'He [Christ] is not a human being but is like a human being, since he is not coessential with humanity in his highest part' (*On the Union in Christ*).[4] This is very similar to an earlier heresy in church history called Docetism, according to which Jesus only 'appears' (Greek *dokeō*) to be human.

It was one of the Cappadocian bishops, Gregory of Nazianzus, who, like Athanasius with Arius, responded that such a

---

4   In Edward T. Oakes, *Infinity Dwindled to Infancy: A Catholic and Evangelical Christology* (Grand Rapids: Eerdmans, 2011), footnote on p. 137.

conception would jeopardize our salvation. He coined a slogan which pinpointed the fundamental problem: 'That which he has not assumed he has not healed but what is united to the Godhead is thereby saved' (*Epistle 101 to Cledonius*).[5] In contrast to Gnosticism or Greek notions of 'afterlife', the biblical contention is that salvation is holistic. It is not that matter is evil and so the body has to be shed to release the 'soul' which is imprisoned, in which case Christ need only have taken to himself a human spirit. Rather, whatever constitutes a human being is required to be redeemed *in toto* for a full salvation to be accomplished. This is in line with the writer to the Hebrews:

> Since children have flesh and blood, he too shared in their humanity [which 'flesh and blood' refers to] so that by his death he might break the power of him who holds the power of death – that is, the devil – and free those who all their lives were held in slavery by their fear of death.
> (Heb. 2:14–15 NIV)

This is essentially the theological point Gregory was making.

Again we see how the major doctrines are interlinked. Christology (who Jesus is) determines soteriology (how Jesus saves).

Gregory of Nazianzus's argument won the day and Apollinaris was condemned at the First Council of Constantinople in 381.[6]

---

5 Cited in Kelly M. Kapic, 'Anthropology', in Michael Allen and Scott R. Swain (eds.), *Christian Dogmatics: Reformed Theology for the Church Catholic* (Grand Rapids: Baker Academic, 2016), p. 173.

6 For a helpful and clear presentation of the issues, see Oakes, *Infinity Dwindled to Infancy*.

Jesus is one person: Ephesus, AD 431

Having affirmed the full deity and full humanity of Christ at the first two councils, the question of how the two were to be understood as relating to each other led to another heresy: 'adoptionism', according to which Jesus was a human like us but at some point was 'adopted' by the Father to *become* his Son.

A subtle form of this heresy appeared in the teaching of a bishop of Constantinople called Nestorius.

Meaning well doesn't always end well

Here we have an example of good intentions leading to bad theology.

As far as good intentions were concerned, Nestorius wanted to ensure that the integrity of the humanity of Christ was maintained. For this to be so, two things, in his view, were essential. First, the humanity of Christ had to be complete, and this included his possessing a rational soul or intellect. Second, both the humanity and the divinity of Christ would be compromised if each did not keep their essential characteristics. This, he argued, meant that each nature had its respective *prosōpon*, which some took to mean 'person' or 'personality'.[7]

Nestorius wrestled with the idea that Christ was divine from birth, stating, 'I could not call a two or three month old baby God.'[8] In Nestorius's mind there was a radical disjunction between the divine nature and the human nature:

---

7 D. F. Wells is charitable in his presentation of Nestorius's ideas that he was using the term more elastically, such that just as a face (*prosōpon*) reveals the mood or character of the person, so Christ, 'in what he said and did, revealed both his humanity and his divinity'. D. F. Wells, *The Person of Christ: A Biblical and Historical Analysis of the Incarnation* (Wheaton: Crossway, 1984), p. 107.

8 Cited in Tony Lane, *Exploring Christian Doctrine* (London: SPCK, 2013), p. 133.

Divine attributes	Human attributes
Gives life	Born
Is everywhere	Grows
Knows all	Learns
Rules in glory	Suffers
Eternal	Dies

Nestorius was taken to task by Cyril the Bishop of Alexandria.[9] He argued that to understand the person of Jesus aright it was possible to take a subject from the one category and the predicate (a statement made *about* the subject) from another and bring them together, because both sets of attributes are true of the one person, the Son Jesus Christ. Thus the one who gives life as only God can do is *also* the one who is born into the world (thus the pairing: Gives life – Born). The one who knows all things (omniscient) is also the one who in Jesus grows in knowledge (Knows all – Learns). God is impassable (not subject to change or suffering) but in Jesus he suffered (Rules in glory – Suffers). This exchange of attributes between the human and the divine was known as the *communicatio idiomatum*. In the one person of the Son made flesh, the two sets of attributes meet.

Of course, this was something to which earlier theologians also held. Here, for example, is the mystical Semitic writer Ephraim (d. 373):

---

9 The idea of a 'two-nature theory' was not original to Nestorius. It had been developed by an earlier opponent of Apollinaris, Theodore of Mopsuestia (*c*.350–428). He argued that predicates pertaining to divinity could *only* be applied to divinity, and predicates pertaining to humanity could *only* be applied to humanity. And so when Christ wept, that was his human nature at work, but when he performed miracles, that was the work of his divine nature. This led to some very muddled interpretation of Scripture so that according to Theodore, when Jesus said, 'I come from the Father', that was divinity speaking, but when he said, 'I go to the Father', that was his humanity speaking!

He was silent as a babe, and yet He was making His creatures execute all His commands ... The thirty years He
was in the earth, Who was ordering all creatures, Who
was receiving offerings of praise from those above and
those below ... While the Conception of the Son was
fashioning in the womb, He Himself was fashioning
babes in the womb. Yet not as His body was weak in the
womb, was His power weak in the womb! So too not as
His body was feeble by the Cross, was His might also
feeble by the Cross. For when on the Cross He quickened
the dead, His Body quickened them, yea, rather His Will;
just as when He was wholly dwelling in the womb, His
hidden Will was visiting all![10]

'God-bearer'

Following through the *communicatio idiomatum*, Cyril of
Alexandria spoke of Mary, the mother of Jesus, as *theotokos* –
literally, 'God-bearer', or, as it was also rendered, 'mother of
God', which Nestorius strenuously objected to. At this point
the issue was not the status of Mary (after all, to speak of
Mary as 'mother of God' suggests some kind of seniority, as
seen in later developments in terms of Catholic Mariolatry)
but the identity of Jesus. *Theotokos* was a shorthand
declaration that the baby born of Mary was truly Emmanuel,
God with us.

Although Nestorius's view is sometimes referred to as 'two-
natured' Christology, what one ends up with is more like
having 'two persons' in one body. After all, natures don't choose

10 *Hymns on the Nativity of Christ in the Flesh* 3, in Philip Schaff, *A Select Library of Nicene
and Post-Nicene Fathers of the Christian Church*, Series 2, vol. 13 (New York: Christian
Literature Co., 1886–1900), p. 427.

(e.g. to desire the cup of suffering to pass or to accept it – Mark 14:36f.); rather, *persons* do the choosing. So it would seem, with Nestorius, that a model of Christ is conceived whereby there is a duality of *persons* within Christ, one divine and one human, who have to work out a course of action between themselves. It conjures up in the mind the kind of duality you have in a pantomime horse. Externally it looks as if it is one entity, but inside there are two people trying to work out things together so it at least looks like there is only one horse going in one direction!

Cyril's solution cut through the confusion: the eternal Logos who is one with the Father (*homoousios*) is the *active subject* (person) who takes on perfect human nature. So whatever can be said of one of his natures (whether it be divine or human) can be said about *him*, the Logos Jesus Christ. He is, after all, the Word become flesh (*God* became *human*). The 'I' that said 'I thirst' is the same 'I' that said 'Before Abraham was, I am.' There is no room for Nestorian schizophrenia. This union of the person of the Logos (*hypostasis*) with human nature in Jesus is referred to as the *hypostatic* union.[11]

The church sided with Cyril in this debate and Nestorius was deposed in 431 and his views repudiated as heresy.

Establishing the two natures of Christ: Chalcedon, AD 451

We finally come to someone else who took a theological position to an extreme, a monk from Constantinople called

---

11 That is, the human nature of Christ is both anhypostatic (not personal in itself) and enhypostatic (personalized by union with the eternal person of the Son). See Sanders, 'Chalcedonian Categories', p. 31.

Eutyches in 449. In this case it was Cyril's theology which was stretched in a particular direction until it snapped.

Cyril fought to establish that in Christ there was one *person* (the Logos) as the active principle. Eutyches pushed this further towards Christ having only one *nature*. He was not going to reduce this to Christ having either only a divine nature (and so end up in a position like Apollinaris) or only a human nature (and so finding himself in a position similar to Arius). Rather, as a result of the incarnation there was a *mixing* of the divine and the human natures into a *third* nature, a divine–human nature, what is called a *tertium quid*, a third 'something' which is neither one nor the other. We may think of it like this: imagine the divine nature being represented by the colour blue and the human nature by the colour green. Mix them together and what is the result? Yellow! The upshot is that Jesus is neither fully God nor fully man. And by now you will have worked out that this, too, puts our salvation at risk, for only God can save and only a man can represent humanity, and Jesus on this reckoning is neither!

In fact, the result is probably more subtle than the mixing of colours. If the divine nature is qualitatively infinite compared with the human nature, the result is more of a divine than a human Christ.[12] Again, think of an analogy. If one were to take a bucket full of fresh water (representing the human nature of Christ) and place it into the Atlantic Ocean (representing the divine nature), what happens to the fresh water/human nature? It becomes absorbed by the sea water/divine.

The heresy of Eutychianism can be represented diagrammatically as follows:

---

12 Sanders, 'Chalcedonian Categories', p. 22.

```
Godhood              Manhood
XXXXXXXX             +++++++++
```

```
        United in the incarnation
        X+X+X+X+X+X+X+X+X+X          A third 'nature'
```

At Chalcedon such a view was roundly repudiated, anathematizing 'those who imagine a mixture or confusion of the two natures of Christ' and also 'those who, first idly talk of the natures of the Lord as "two before the union" and then conceive but "one after the union"'.[13]

The orthodox view is represented by a saying of Gregory of Nazianzus: 'What he [Christ] was he remained, what he was not he became' (Gregory had a knack for coming up with a snappy theological sound bite!).

Diagrammatically, the Chalcedonian formulation could be represented like this:

```
                    Godhood
                    XXXXXXXXXXX
Incarnation----------------------------------------------------------------
            Godhood-----Person of Christ-----Manhood
            XXXXXXX                          ++++++++
```

This is the way it is expressed in the Chalcedonian Definition itself:

> He was begotten before all ages from the Father as regards his divinity, and in the last days the same for us and for our salvation from Mary, the virgin God-bearer, as regards his humanity; one and the same Christ, Son, Lord,

---

13 Sanders, 'Chalcedonian Categories', p. 22.

only-begotten, acknowledged in two natures which undergo no confusion, no change, no division, no separation; at no point was the difference between the natures taken away through the union, but rather the property of both natures is preserved and comes together into a single person and single subsistent being . . .[14]

The 'Chalcedonian Box'

We have seen how the early church sought to carefully negotiate the high-wire balancing act with regards to the person of Christ. Whilst no doubt political and cultural factors (as well as personal ones) were at play during the great Christological debates, the formulations themselves are first and foremost theological, a serious attempt to do justice to the biblical witness. We have also seen that in each case it was not a matter of ensuring the triumph of a particular church 'party' but salvation itself that was of supreme concern. Jesus said, 'If you hold to my teaching, you are really my disciples. Then you will know the truth, and the truth will set you free' (John 8:32 NIV). It was a desire to hold to Christ's teaching and so the truth which often led to intense and passionate debate. Not only was Christ's honour at stake, but also people's salvation, and this could not be allowed to be whittled away by compromise.

The theological boundaries laid down at Chalcedon which excluded erroneous views and permitted considered debate within acceptable parameters have been represented by Fred Sanders as the 'Chalcedonian Box' (see Figure 1 on p. 122).[15] This helpfully summarizes what we have been exploring in this

---

14 Cited in Sanders, 'Chalcedonian Categories', p. 23.
15 Sanders, 'Chalcedonian Categories', p. 24.

First Council: Nicaea (AD 325)
Condemned Arianism.
Soteriological axiom: 'God alone can save us'

FULLY GOD

ONE PERSON

TWO NATURES

Third Council:
Ephesus (AD 431)
Condemned Nestorianism.
Specified the one
person of Christ

Fourth Council:
Chalcedon (AD 451)
Condemned Eutychianism.
Maintained the two natures
without confusion or change,
separation or division

FULLY HUMAN

Second Council:
Constantinople I (AD 381)
Reaffirmed Nicaea, condemned Apollinarianism.
Soteriological axiom: 'That which is not assumed is
not healed'

Figure 1 **The 'Chalcedonian Box'**

chapter. As has been noted, it is a powerful, evangelical statement of the Christian claim 'that our Lord Jesus Christ, who was crucified in his human flesh, is truly God and the Lord of glory and one of the members of the Trinity'.[16]

Questions for reflection and discussion

- Where in the 'Chalcedonian Box' was your understanding of Christ? How, if at all, has it changed in the light of our discussion?
- How is the doctrine of the incarnation (Christology) related to the doctrine of salvation (soteriology)? How does one affect the other?
- Why is it possible to worship Jesus who was a man without committing blasphemy?

16 Sanders, 'Chalcedonian Categories', p. 36.

Prayer

Almighty God, who hast given us thy only-begotten Son to take our nature upon him, and as at this time to be born of a pure Virgin: Grant that we being regenerate, and made thy children by adoption and grace, may daily be renewed by thy Holy Spirit; through the same our Lord Jesus Christ, who liveth and reigneth with thee and the same Spirit, ever one God, world without end. Amen.

(Book of Common Prayer, Collect for Christmas Day)

9

The mind of Christ

In his 'Essay on Criticism', the eighteenth-century poet Alexander Pope spoke of fools rushing in 'where angels fear to tread'. Early on in the life of the church, Hilary of Poitiers in the fourth century issued a similar warning with regard to theological enquiry:

> The guilt of the heretics and blasphemers compels us to undertake what is unlawful, to scale arduous heights, to speak of the ineffable, and to trespass upon forbidden places. And since by faith alone we should fulfil what is commanded, namely, to adore the Father, to venerate the Son with Him, and to abound in the Holy Spirit, we are forced to raise our lowly words to subjects that cannot be described. By the guilt of another we are forced into guilt, so that what should have been restricted to the pious contemplation of our minds is now exposed to the dangers of human speech.
>
> (*On the Trinity* 2.2)[1]

This is a salutary warning against presumptuous theorizing which runs the danger of spilling over into heresy. The humble acknowledgment of Job after he had wrestled with some deep

---

1   Cited by Paul Helm, 'Taking a Line IV: A Time to Keep Silence', Helm's Deep (blog), 14 December 2008, <https://paulhelmsdeep.blogspot.com/2008/12/taking-line-iv-time-to-keep-silence.html>.

mysteries of his own is one which should constantly be borne in mind: 'Surely I spoke of things I did not understand, things too wonderful for me to know' (Job 42:3 NIV).

We have certainly been delving into things 'too wonderful' to know in relation to the incarnation of the eternal Son of God. Perhaps this is where we should leave things, as Charles Wesley put it, 'lost in wonder, love and praise'? That would not be an inappropriate response.

And yet . . . Whilst bearing in mind the warning of St Hilary, and without rushing in like a fool, could we not tentatively explore things a little further to try to gain *some* understanding, however limited, of the way the two natures united in the one person of Christ might relate?

The story so far

We have seen that by the time we get to Chalcedon certain 'givens' have been established with regard to the person of Jesus Christ.

First of all, the second person of the Trinity, the divine Logos, is eternally a person with a divine nature. He is co-equal and co-eternal with the Father.

Second, at the incarnation those properties which define human nature were assumed by the Logos and so are exemplified by a divine person. Jesus is fully human. An actual person is an individual with a nature for, as DeWeese points out, there are no 'denatured persons'. The nature 'determines the kind of person it is'.[2] The Son prior to the incarnation solely had a

---

2 Garrett J. DeWeese, 'One Person, Two Natures: Two Metaphysical Models of the Incarnation', in Fred Sanders and Klaus Issler (eds.), *Jesus in Trinitarian Perspective* (Nashville: Broadman & Holman, 2007), p. 142.

divine nature. Consequent upon the incarnation the Son has a divine *and* human nature. The latter, according to J. O. Buswell, means that the eternal Son 'took to himself a human volitional behaviour pattern when he took to himself all the essential attributes of human nature'.[3]

In becoming a man, the Son does not give up his divine nature; he assumes a human nature, a 'new mode of existence, and so makes human experiences his own'.[4] Or, as summarized by Thomas Weinandy, 'Jesus is the *person* of the Son *existing* as a man.'[5]

Thinking inside the box

In the last chapter we saw that Fred Sanders' 'Chalcedonian Box' provides the boundaries for proper, regulated theological thought about the person of Christ. However, within that box, what are we to make of some of the statements relating to the life of Jesus as we find them in the Gospels? For example, in John 4 we find Jesus tired from his journey and so he sits at the side of Jacob's well at Sychar. Does this mean that God gets tired or sits? Later in the same Gospel we find Jesus beside the grave of Lazarus and we are told that he 'wept'. Are we right to conclude, therefore, that God weeps? Of course, one may try to deal with such questions by saying that it is only as the *man* Jesus that God tires and weeps, and that God-in-himself does not and cannot (however, such a position veers in the

---

3 Cited by T. L. Tiessen, 'Of What Did the Son of God Empty Himself in Becoming Human?', Thoughts Theological (blog), 6 January 2017, <http://www.thoughtstheological.com/of-what-did-the-son-of-god-empty-himself-in-becoming-human/>.

4 Kevin J. Vanhoozer, 'Impassible Passion', in *Remythologizing Theology: Divine Action, Passion and Authorship* (Cambridge: Cambridge University Press, 2010), p. 423.

5 Thomas G. Weinandy, *Does God Suffer?* (Paris: University of Notre Dame Press, 2000), p. 175.

direction of Nestorianism). Perhaps more problematic is Jesus' prayer in Mark 14 and the agony of Gethsemane, 'Abba, Father, all things are possible for you. Remove this cup from me. Yet not what I will, but what you will.' Does this mean that Jesus has a will which is at variance, however slight, with that of his Father, or that within Jesus himself there is some sort of conflict between his divine will (which is one with the Father's) and his human will (in which case we are back to Nestorianism)?

Whose will?

The matter of Jesus' will needs to be teased out a little further as it became a major bone of contention within the church in the sixth and seventh centuries and is still very much with us.[6] The belief that there is only one God would seem to require that eternally there is one will within the Godhead. That is not the area of debate we are considering, although it is related. Our aim is to explore how we might come to understand the will of the Son *incarnate*, the one who is human and divine.

The technical terms used in this debate are *monothelitism*, which is the view that Jesus had only one will, and *dyothelitism*, that he had two wills – one which was divine and one which was human.

The Chalcedonian formulation appeared to be ambiguous on this matter, as Adolf Harnack observed: 'The doctrine of one will equally with that of two wills would have been in harmony with the decisions of the Fourth and Fifth Councils [Chalcedon

---

6 For a helpful presentation of the different viewpoints, ancient and modern, see Stephen J. Wellum, *God the Son Incarnate* (Wheaton: Crossway, 2016), pp. 338–348.

and Constantinople]."[7] Clarity was sought at the Sixth Ecumenical Council (the Third Council of Constantinople, 680–681), which condemned monothelitism and affirmed that Christ had both a divine and a human will. Some have argued that this was mainly a matter of the church closing the door on Monophysitism or Eutychianism (the belief that Christ had only one nature) as there was an attempt to sneak in the error by a different path (Christ having only one will); nonetheless, the intention of the council in fending off this error could have been upheld without it entailing dyothelitism.[8] It would seem that both positions seek to do justice to Chalcedon. The monothelites' desire is to ensure that Nestorianism is avoided: that Christ is not divided into two persons, which 'two wills' might seem to suggest. The dyothelites, on the other hand, wish to preserve the two natures of Christ, which, depending upon one's understanding of 'nature', would appear to imply having a divine will and a human will (for without 'wills' one or both natures would be incomplete).

Perhaps we should have listened to St Hilary after all and let things be!

However, let's not throw up our hands in despair just yet. Drawing on the insights of some modern theologians,[9] we

---

7 Adolf von Harnack, *History of Dogma* (3rd edn; trans. Neil Buchanan; Boston: Little, Brown, 1898), 4:254. DeWeese points out that the Chalcedonian tradition was not clear on this as it had simply not come up. DeWeese, 'One Person, Two Natures', p. 123.

8 Tiessen, 'Of What Did the Son of God Empty Himself?'

9 R. L. Sturch, 'The Metaphysics of the Incarnation', *Vox Evangelica* 10 (1977), pp. 65–76; DeWeese, 'One Person, Two Natures', pp. 114–153; William Lane Craig, 'The Incarnation', in J. P. Moreland and William Lane Craig (eds.), *Philosophical Foundations for a Christian World View* (London: Inter-Varsity Press, 2017), pp. 595–611; Vanhoozer, 'Impassible Passion', pp. 387–433. The position being advanced by DeWeese and Craig has been described as Functional Kenotic Christology (FKC). A moderate and qualified defence of FKC is found in Tiessen, 'Of What Did the Son of God Empty Himself?' What is proposed in this chapter is one way of looking at the relation between the person of Christ and the two natures which *selectively* draws on the insights of FKC to form a model which remains within the 'Chalcedonian Box'.

might tentatively work towards a model for understanding how the personhood of the Son might operate within the constraints of the human nature of Jesus.[10] It must be stressed, however, that by definition this will be speculative, maybe highly so, and if in reading this you feel it is not convincing, then it can be set aside without any great loss. If, on the other hand, you find it suggestive, all well and good, so long as sight is not lost of the non-negotiable doctrines which are enveloped by the 'Chalcedonian Box'.

The divine condescension

We saw in chapter 7 in the great 'song' to Christ of Philippians 2:6–11 the centrality of the Son's 'emptying' (*ekenōsen*), whereby a glorious humbling of God took place, not in the sense of the *giving up* of any of his 'godness', but by his *taking on* of humanness – the 'form of a man'. May this not also suggest a 'self-limitation' in the 'self-emptying': the Son embracing the limitations of a sinless yet human nature? This would mean that during his incarnate ministry on earth, the Son voluntarily restricted the exercise of those capacities of his personhood to the range of thoughts (using logic – moving from premises to conclusions etc.), perceptions (seeing, hearing, smelling, touching), sensations (joy, pain, weariness) and volitions (making choices to do and not do things) which would be exercised by a person operating within the normal limitations of sinless human nature. Jesus would gain information about

---

10 John Frame believes there is room for such thinking not only to develop theology proper but also to foster edification: 'I think that godly speculation can have an edifying function.' John M. Frame, *The Doctrine of God* (Phillipsburg: Presbyterian and Reformed, 2002), p. 725. The key word is 'godly'.

the world, and indeed God's dealings with and plans for the world, through the body's normal gathering processes and faculties, that is, reading and meditating on the Old Testament Scriptures, learning how to make tables out of wood, the storing of memories through the instrumentality of the brain, and so on. In short, the Son lived a perfect human life in delightful loving obedience to his heavenly Father in complete dependence upon the Holy Spirit.

In two minds?

Recognizing that when it comes to speaking of divine mysteries we will be stretching language to the limit (but hopefully not *beyond* the limit into error), we are not to imagine that Jesus had two minds – a divine mind and a human mind. Rather, what is being envisaged is that the human mind of Jesus is the *mode of operation* of the mind of the Son functioning within the constraints of Jesus' human nature and body. *At the same time*, the mind of the Son, functioning gloriously and perfectly according to the divine nature, 'never sleeps, and never ceases to be omniscient'.[11]

If we are not saying that Jesus had two minds – one human and one divine – how, then, might we begin to think of the way the mind of the Son (or divine consciousness) relates to the mind embodied in the brain of Jesus (human consciousness)?

One way of conceiving this has been suggested by William Lane Craig.[12] Drawing on 'depth psychology' and the idea that there is vastly more to a person than waking consciousness, Craig speaks of the 'subliminal self' as being the primary

---

11 DeWeese, 'One Person, Two Natures', p. 146.
12 Craig, 'Incarnation', pp. 595–611.

location of the superhuman elements in the consciousness of the incarnate Logos. This means that while Jesus experienced a normal human consciousness, that consciousness was underlain by a *divine subconscious*. This is in line with the suggestion of DeWeese that the human mind is a kind of 'subset' of the divine mind, as well as the view of Sturch that the 'self' which undergoes the joys and pains of Jesus of Nazareth is the same 'self' of the Logos, what he calls the 'substantival self'.[13]

Let's follow Craig's proposal and see where it leads.

As outlined above, taking our cue from Philippians 2, during the state of his humbling in the incarnation the Logos allowed only those facets of his person that were compatible with human experience to be part of Christ's waking consciousness, 'while the bulk of his knowledge and other cognitive perfections, like an iceberg beneath the water's surface, lay submerged in his subconscious'.[14] Since a *person* has a mind and a will and a nature does not, Christ had *one* mind and *one* will which belonged to the divine person.[15] Craig argues that this model avoids the errors of Nestorianism because it 'does not imply that there are two persons any more than the conscious aspect of one's life and the subconscious aspect of one's life constitute two people'.[16]

---

13 Sturch, 'Metaphysics of the Incarnation', p. 74.
14 Craig, 'Incarnation', p. 608.
15 DeWeese, 'One Person, Two Natures', p. 144. However, the Third Council of Constantinople in AD 681 affirmed that for the Son to have a true human nature he had to have a human will. One of the main advocates of this position was Maximus the Confessor who argued that the 'will' referring to the *process* of *willing* belonged to the level of natures. Thus for Christ to have a fully divine and fully human nature he must have two wills pertaining to each nature; see Andrew Ter Ern Loke, 'On Dyothelitism versus Monothelitism: The Divine Preconscious Model', *The Heythrop Journal* 57 (2016), pp. 136–137, <https://onlinelibrary.wiley.com/doi/epdf/10.1111/heyj.12073>.
16 Craig, 'Incarnation', p. 608.

Craig maintains that this model does justice to the data of the Gospels:

> In his conscious experience, Jesus grew in knowledge and wisdom, just as a human child does. One does not have the monstrosity of the baby Jesus lying in the manger possessing full divine consciousness ... In his waking consciousness, Jesus is actually ignorant of certain facts, though kept from error and often supernaturally illumined by the divine subliminal. Even though the Logos possesses all knowledge about the world from quantum mechanics to auto mechanics, there is no reason to think that Jesus of Nazareth would have been able to answer questions about such subjects, so low had he stooped in condescending to take on the human condition.

He goes on,

> Moreover, in his conscious life, Jesus knew the whole gamut of human anxieties and felt hurt and fatigue. The model also preserves the integrity and sincerity of Jesus' prayer life, and it explains why Jesus was capable of being perfected through suffering. He, like us, needed to be dependent on his Father moment by moment in order to live victoriously in a fallen world and to carry out successfully the mission with which he had been charged.[17]

---

17 Craig, 'Incarnation', p. 609. This was also what Cyril of Alexandria held with his idea of the *communicatio idiomatum*: 'We ought to touch on the divine plan and remark that God's only-begotten Word took on along with humanity all its attributes save sin alone.

One obvious question mark raised against Craig's talk of a 'divine subconscious' is that it gives the impression that during the Son of God's incarnation, the divine consciousness was in some state of 'stasis' or inactivity, a passive reservoir which is occasionally 'tapped' by the Son in his temporal state. This would not sit easily with the doctrine we mentioned in chapter 2 and which we shall be exploring in more depth in the next chapter, that while incarnate, nonetheless the eternal Son was active throughout the universe. So whatever 'divine subconscious' may have existed in the person of Jesus of Nazareth, this is not to be construed as some kind of passive unconsciousness.[18]

Sturch, using more technical philosophical language, ends up at the same point as William Lane Craig and DeWeese.[19]

Ignorance of future events properly belongs to the limitations of humanity and so, in so far as he is viewed as God, he knows all that the Father knows; in so far, though, as the same Son of Man, he does not repudiate the appearance of ignorance because it is an attribute of humanity. Just as he who is personally the Life and Power of all took bodily nourishment out of respect for the measure of his self-emptying and is recorded to have slept and been weary, so, though knowing all things, he was not ashamed to allot himself the ignorance which belongs to humanity, because his were all the attributes of humanity save sin alone.' Cyril of Alexandria, *Answers to Tiberias* 4.

18 Craig's proposals have been subject to criticism by Wellum, *God the Son Incarnate*, pp. 380–409, and Donald Macleod in his review of Wellum's book, 'Your Go-To Book on the Doctrine of Christ', The Gospel Coalition, 23 December 2016, <https://www.thegospelcoalition.org/reviews/god-the-son-incarnate/>.

19 'If the human "centre" is that which has all a human being's experiences (in the widest possible sense, including actions, desires and so on), then the expression "A human centre" does not mean "A centre of the particular type we call 'human'" but "A centre with human experiences inhering in it". Similarly, a divine "centre" is a centre of divine experiences, not one of a special divine type. We might illustrate the point by a diagram consisting of two squares touching one another at a corner. The geometrical point at which they meet is a corner of both squares, yet neither square lacks any necessary feature. We cannot say that the smaller "human" square is in some way incomplete; nor for that matter that the larger "divine" one is. We might note in passing that this understanding of the union fits the later doctrine of the "enhypostasia". The experiencing centre - what corresponds on this view to the hypostasis of the Fathers, whether or not they meant anything like it by that word - already existed as the hypostasis of God the Son before the Incarnation, and no new centre of being had to be created for the man Jesus of Nazareth.' Sturch, 'Metaphysics of the Incarnation', p. 75.

To offset any suggestion that in his incarnation Jesus was operationally no different from a mere 'Spirit-filled man', we might think of the instances where Jesus displays supernatural knowledge (e.g. John 1:46–48), divine self-awareness and self-identity (Luke 2:49; Matt. 11:25–27; John 17) and supernatural powers normally attributed to God (Mark 4:39–41; cf. Ps. 89:9). Sturch suggests that according to the kind of model we have been developing,

> Our Lord's miraculous powers and supernatural knowledge would then be communicated to His human life and nature when needed, and His contemporaries were right to see them as signs of prophetic status (Luke 7:16; John 4:19). Hence He could indeed reveal God as God chose, not so much because of His divine status as because of the divine activity in and through Him.

However, this is not to suggest that the Son was a mere passive agent in all of this. In John's Gospel the Son's having life 'in himself' (John 5:26) and having the authority to lay down and take up his life (John 10:18) leads us to say that it is his own divine status as well as the work of the other members of the Trinity in and through him which contributes to these divine displays.[20]

Donald Macleod further unpacks how this might be construed. He suggests that Jesus' experience was in many ways

---

20 Sturch, 'Metaphysics of the Incarnation', p. 75. In reviewing Wellum's book which, as already noted, is critical of DeWeese and Craig, Macleod asserts, 'We must not overlook that the incarnation *did* involve a real kenosis. Some theologians of the strictest Reformed orthodoxy (Scotland's Hugh Martin, for example) were prepared to define this kenosis in terms of his divine attributes being "in abeyance" – not, of course, in relation to his cosmic functions but in relation to the mediatorial ministry he had to perform as the Messiah: incognito, and in servant form.' Macleod, 'Your Go-To Book'.

parallel to our own. The main difference was that he was sinless, which would have meant not only that his intellect was perfectly attuned to the Divine, but that he had a unique intimacy with the Father:

> He conversed with God as his Son; and he thought as his Son. We may even say that he lived in a thought-world of pure revelation so that to an extent we cannot fathom God disclosed himself not only to his thinking but *in* his thinking. In this respect, revelation, in the case of Christ, was concurrent with his own thought-processes.[21]

In assessing Craig's position Tiessen concludes,

> The eternal Son of God, conceived in the womb of Mary by the Holy Spirit, added to his person the attributes of humanity in such a way that, though continuing to be only one person, with one will and mind, he now had both the infinitude of divinity and the limitations of humanity. During the time of his humiliation, he never ceased to be divine, but he chose to live in the same dependence upon the Father and the Spirit which should be the experience of all of us descendants of the first Adam.

Tiessen then goes on to draw out the implications for those who are 'in Christ': 'When we are glorified, we will be like Christ in the sense that he was the paradigmatic human after whose

---

21 Donald Macleod, *The Person of Christ*, Contours of Christian Theology (Leicester: Inter-Varsity Press, 1998), p. 167.

image Adam and Eve were created, so we will then be perfectly human, but we will not become divine.'[22]

It would seem that in order to do justice to the 'two natures–one person' Christology of Chalcedon, some kind of 'functional kenosis' (Functional Kenotic Christology, FKC) is unavoidable. This is even detectable in Wellum, who is one of the most ardent critics of the position we have been outlining. In his blog post for The Gospel Coalition entitled '10 Things You Should Know about the Incarnation', item 7 states,

> From conception, the Son limited his divine life in such a way that he did not override the limitations of his human nature. As a result of the incarnation, the divine Son lives as a true man with the normal physical, mental, volitional, and psychological attributes and capacities of original humanity. As the incarnate Son, he experienced the wonder and weaknesses of a completely human life. He grew in wisdom and physical stature (Luke 2:52), experienced tears and joy, and suffered death and a glorious resurrection for his people's salvation (John 11:33, 35; 19:30; 1 Cor. 15:3–4).[23]

This smacks of functional kenosis in all but name.

Thy will be done

One incident in the life of Christ which has caused much consternation when trying to get to grips with the Chalcedonian

---

22 Tiessen, 'Of What Did the Son of God Empty Himself?'
23 Stephen Wellum, '10 Things You Should Know about the Incarnation', The Gospel Coalition, 24 December 2016, <https://www.thegospelcoalition.org/article/10-things-you-should-know-about-the-incarnation/>.

presentation of Christ is the agony of Jesus in Gethsemane, with his desperate request and subsequent submission, 'My Father, if it is possible, may this cup be taken from me. Yet not as I will, but as you will' (Matt. 26:39 NIV). The traditional way of interpreting this is by attributing two wills to Christ according to the two natures (which some argue carries echoes of Nestorianism). Such an interpretation might run along the following lines:

> The human will of Christ's human nature desired the cup to pass, but his divine will (which was numerically identical with the Father's will) did not and it is the divine will which controls Jesus' decision making, so there is no possibility that human desires are acted upon. While normally the divine will in Christ so overpowers his human will that the human will is invisible, on this one occasion we are privileged to see it.[24]

But if it is *persons* who will, and not natures, this won't do, otherwise we have moved outside the 'Chalcedonian Box' significantly to the left and we more or less end up as Nestorians.

Here we need to be a little more precise when we speak of someone's 'will'. It could mean one of two things: 'that which is desired' as distinct from the 'exercise of active power'.[25] Thus in the unity of the Trinity, what the Father wills and the Son wills and the Spirit wills are one in terms of 'that which is desired' (the creation of a world, the redemption of people, etc.). But according to our model, when Jesus prayed 'not as I will, but as you will', the *one* personal will of Christ, operating as a

---

24 DeWeese, 'One Person, Two Natures', p. 151.
25 DeWeese, 'One Person, Two Natures', p. 150.

human person, willed (that is, humanly *desired*) for the cup to pass. But he exercised his *active will* in submitting to the desired will of his Father (which is also, of course, what he, the eternal Son, and the Spirit desired: 'will' in the first sense).[26] As Craig puts it,

[Christ's prayers in the garden] do not contemplate a struggle of Jesus' human will with his divine will (he is not, after all, talking to himself!), but have reference to the interaction between Jesus' will ('my will') and the Father's ('your will'). Possessing a typical human consciousness, Jesus had to struggle against fear, weakness and temptation in order to align his will with that of his heavenly Father. The will of the Logos had in virtue of the Incarnation become the will of the man Jesus of Nazareth.[27]

---

26 'When Jesus says, "Not my will but yours be done," he is by the exercise of his own active power submitting his natural desire to avoid the coming agony to the desire of the Father, and the coming exercise of the Father's active power.' DeWeese, 'One Person, Two Natures', p. 151.

27 Craig, 'Incarnation', p. 608. A not too dissimilar construal has been proposed more recently by Andrew Ter Ern Loke. Holding to a dyothelite position, he develops a 'Divine Preconscious Model' (DPM) of the incarnation, which he describes in the following way: 'According to this model, at the incarnation the conscious mind of the Logos came to include a consciousness and a preconscious, and certain divine properties such as the knowledge of all truths resided in the preconscious (the preconscious is understood as mental contents in the subconscious that are not currently in consciousness but are accessible to consciousness by directing attention to them). At the same time, a human preconscious and a human body were created. In addition, the consciousness acquired human properties that were also newly created. This acquisition included a certain extent of the consciousness' capacity to function being made dependent on the brain, resulting in the capacity to experience physical pain, to have sensations through physical organs, and to have the desires for food, for sleep, etc. DPM is thus a form of Functional Kenoticism: the Logos continued to possess divine properties (e.g. omniscience, omnipotence) in his divine preconscious after incarnation, but he chose not to use these divine powers in certain acts that he performed.' Andrew Ter Ern Loke, 'On Dyothelitism versus Monothelitism', pp. 135–141. He concludes, 'The result is that the motivation of Dyothelites (to ensure the completeness of the human and divine natures) as well as the concern of Monothelites (to ensure that there is no division of Christ into two persons) can both be met.' I am grateful to Dr Philip Duce for drawing my attention to this article.

Divine suffering?

The model we have been pursuing concerning the person of Christ also does justice to Cyril's notion of *communicatio idiomatum* in relation to the suffering of Jesus.[28] Natures, as such, do not suffer, because to speak of something's 'nature' is to refer to the *kind* of thing it is, its 'whatness' – for example, the animal nature of Fido the pet dog. Natures do not have a concrete existence on their own *apart* from individuals. An actual person is an individual *together with a nature*. As we have seen, according to the Chalcedonian Definition, the person of Jesus of Nazareth (the individual) has two natures, human and divine. And so when we think of the suffering of Jesus, we don't assign suffering either to his human nature or to his divine nature, but to the divine *person*.

Cyril argued that the one divine Word exists in two distinct states: unincarnate (*logos asarkos*) within the framework of what is called the 'immanent Trinity' – that is, eternal; and incarnate (*logos ensarkos*) within the framework of what is called the 'economic Trinity' in history. The Logos, while retaining his divine identity, also assumed human identity as Jesus of Nazareth and in so doing became a man 'of sorrows acquainted with grief'. This is helpfully explained by Vanhoozer:

The Son's experiences in time are nevertheless genuine. When he cries out, 'My God, my God, why have you forsaken me?' the Son experiences real anguish in his human self-consciousness. It is the Son of God who feels pain, precisely as the subject of his human existence. The

---

28 Kevin Vanhoozer develops this idea in 'Impassible Passion', pp. 595–611.

experience of Jesus' death and dying is none other than that of the eternal Son of God. Thanks to his humanity, then, the Son is able to 'feel' in time. Such, I submit, is the implication of the *communicatio idiomatum*: the temporal experiences of Jesus Christ are to be assigned neither to his abstract human nature, nor to the divine nature, but rather to a divine person (viz., the Son) in his human mode of existence.[29]

We have already noted that sometimes 'deep' theology is best captured in worshipful song, and so Charles Wesley's classic hymn 'And Can It Be?' is not all that wide of the mark when it declares, ''Tis mystery all, the *immortal* dies.' Cyril would no doubt have approved; after all, this is, in layman's terms, part of what the *communicatio idiomatum* is all about.

Could the Son have sinned?

We briefly turn to another subject regarding the person of Christ which can be explored with some benefit within the 'Chalcedonian Box': the question of how we are to conceive of the sinlessness of Christ.

Some Christians are content to hold the view that Christ was able *not to sin*. This, however, would not particularly distinguish him from the first Adam who had the freedom and the power to do good and refrain from evil. Others, like Jonathan Edwards, believe we must go further and speak of Christ being *not able to sin*:

---

29 Vanhoozer, 'Impassible Passion', p. 425.

It was impossible it should be otherwise, than that he should behave himself holily, and that he should be perfectly holy in each individual act of his life ... it was *impossible* that the Messiah should fail of preserving in integrity and holiness, as the first Adam did.[30]

Here the *communicatio idiomatum* comes to our aid, but in a negative way, marking limitations. As we have seen, the subject 'God' can be linked to many predicates – for example, the Son (the Logos incarnate) may suffer, be tempted, learn and even die – but it *cannot* be said that he could sin, otherwise we have the unthinkable that *God* could sin. Here we are to make an important distinction between Christ being *sinless* (not having sinned or being in a state of sin) and being *impeccable* (unable to sin).

Operating within the 'Chalcedonian Box', W. G. T. Shedd pinpoints why such an idea of the possibility of Christ sinning is in fact an impossibility:

When the Logos goes into union with human nature, so as to constitute a single person with it, he becomes responsible for all that this person does through the instrumentality of this nature ... Should Jesus Christ sin, incarnate God would sin.[31]

Taking as his starting point that with which we began – the self-humbling of Christ – Paul Helm makes an intriguing proposal regarding Christ's impeccability (that Christ cannot sin) which ties in well with the observation of Shedd about

---

30 Cited by Macleod, *Person of Christ*, p. 229.
31 W. G. T. Shedd, *Dogmatic Theology*, vol. 2 (Edinburgh: T&T Clark, 1889), p. 334.

the responsibility of the Logos.[32] Helm suggests that if considered in the abstract, Christ's human nature, being true, unglorified human nature, could sin; but the Mediator, God incarnate, possessing a true human nature, could not sin. He further suggests that part of the humbling of God the Son consists in the Logos *keeping* his human nature from sinning. He so perfectly loves the nature that he has been given that he attends with divine power and grace to it to such a degree that ensures that this human nature can never sin, such that 'There is no possible world in which the incarnate Son sins.'[33]

Helm then goes on to paint a rather moving and delicate picture of what this would mean:

> The Incarnation involves a humbling, like that of a nurse or carer who, by her self-giving, guarantees that her charge can (say) never fall over, and as a perfect human father necessarily keeps his son from being harmed; a person who would, without such care, be harmed. Christ is charged with caring for his human nature by (*inter alia*) keeping it from sinning, and so necessarily he does not sin.

Sinless but fallen?

There is one more issue to consider, and that is whether Christ, though sinless, took to himself a fallen nature in the incarnation. Thomas Torrance is emphatic that he did:

---

32 Paul Helm, 'Crisp Christology', Helm's Deep (blog), 14 April 2010, <https://paulhelmsdeep.blogspot.com/2010/04/crisp-christology.html>.
33 Helm, 'Crisp Christology'.

There can be no doubt that the New Testament speaks of the flesh of Jesus as the concrete form of our human nature marked by Adam's fall ... if Jesus Christ did not assume our fallen flesh, our fallen humanity, then our fallen humanity is not touched by his work – for 'the unassumed is the unredeemed' as Gregory of Nazianzen put it ... Thus Christ took from Mary a corruptible mortal body in order that he might take our sin, judge and condemn it in the flesh, and so assume our human nature as we have it in the fallen world, that he might heal, sanctify and redeem it.[34]

Wellum notes that while the motivation is positive, the argument that Christ took on fallen human nature in order to redeem fallen human beings both misreads the Scriptures and misunderstands the biblical rationale for the incarnation.[35]

From what we have seen so far, Kapic hits the mark when he writes,

Whatever was essential to being human must also be true of the nature assumed by the eternal Son. Accordingly, in the incarnation the eternal Son not only continues to be *homoousios* with the Father in his deity, but the Son also

---

34 Cited in Wellum, *God the Son Incarnate*, p. 232. Karl Barth also adopted this view; e.g. *Church Dogmatics*, 1.2 (trans. G. T. Thompson; Edinburgh: T&T Clark, 1956), p. 153.

35 See Barth, *Church Dogmatics*, 1.2, p. 233. For a more thorough understanding of the debate, see Kelly M. Kapic, 'The Son's Assumption of a Human Nature: A Call for Clarity', *International Journal of Systematic Theology* 3.2 (2001), pp. 154–166; Oliver Crisp, *Divinity and Humanity: The Incarnation Reconsidered* (Cambridge: Cambridge University Press, 2007), pp. 90–117; Ian. A. McFarland, 'Fallen or Unfallen? Christ's Human Nature and the Ontology of Human Sinfulness', *International Journal of Systematic Theology* 10.4 (2008), pp. 399–415.

became *homoousios* with us in our humanity as a result of the assumption of true human nature.[36]

However, this does not necessarily entail *fallen* human nature for it to be *true* human nature. After all, Adam in his pre-fall state was fully human whilst not having a fallen nature. Presumably the redeemed in glory will have glorified sinless bodies without this in any way detracting from their essential humanity. It is true *humanity* which has to be taken on for salvation to be achieved.

This leads us to what can be called the misappropriation of the saying by Gregory Nazianzus, 'the unassumed is the unredeemed', for he also said, 'For all our sakes [the Son] became all that we are, sin apart – body, soul, mind, all that sin pervades.'[37] What Nazianzus is affirming is that the Logos had to take to himself full humanity for full humanity to be redeemed, yet the qualifier 'sin apart' suggests that he did not consider a fallen body – a body which ordinarily 'sin pervades' – to be necessary for this to be so. As Wellum remarks, 'At stake was whether Christ had a full human nature, not whether that nature was fallen.'[38]

Perhaps the most serious objection stems from an understanding of what a fallen human nature entails in terms of its sinful status. A Reformed understanding of this is expressed by the First Confession of Basel (1534): 'Our [fallen] nature [is now] *enfeebled* and became so *inclined to sin* that, unless it is restored by the Spirit of God, man neither does nor wants

---

36 Kelly M. Kapic, 'Anthropology', in Michael Allen and Scott R. Swain (eds.), *Christian Dogmatics: Reformed Theology for the Church Catholic* (Grand Rapids: Baker Academic, 2016), p. 173.
37 Cited in Kapic, 'Anthropology', p. 176.
38 Kapic, 'Anthropology', p. 235.

anything good of himself' (emphasis mine).[39] If this is a faithful summary of the Bible's understanding of fallen human nature, then it is very difficult to see how Jesus could be considered to have a fallen human nature and to be sinless at the same time. The Confession speaks of being 'inclined to sin', and certainly the view of the Puritans was that temptations which come from 'within' (inclined to sin) are themselves sinful. This turns on a particular understanding of what constitutes temptation. Here is John Owen:

> It [temptation] is raising up in the heart, and proposing unto the mind and affections, that which is evil; trying, as it were, whether the soul will close with its suggestions, or how far it will carry them on, though it do not wholly prevail. Now, when such a temptation comes from without, it is unto the soul an indifferent thing, neither good nor evil, unless it be consented unto; *but the very proposal from within, it being the soul's own act, is its sin.* (*Works* 6.194)[40]

Similarly John Davenant writes, '[A]lthough the faculty of desire itself is not sin, yet the inclination and propensity of it to evil is sin; even in one asleep, when it does not at all actually incline to sin.'[41] If this is the case then a non-fallen humanity in the incarnation is a necessary condition for Christ to be Saviour.[42]

---

39 At Apostles-Creed.org, <http://apostles-creed.org/wp-content/uploads/2014/09/The-First-Confession-of-Basel-1534.pdf>.

40 Emphasis mine. See Todd Pruitt, 'Same Sex Attraction, Temptation, and Jesus', Mortification of Spin, 3 August 2018, <http://www.alliancenet.org/mos/1517/same-sex-attraction-temptation-and-jesus#.W3wbLuS0Xx8>.

41 Pruitt, 'Same Sex Attraction'.

42 Applying this principle to Jesus and the question of sexual attraction, Pruitt writes, 'Our temptations typically arise from within us, as we are lured away by desires that give birth to sins such as unbelief and sinful lust (James 1:14–15). Jesus was free from

From warning to worship

We began the chapter with a salutary warning by Hilary of Poitiers concerning the dangers of theological speculation. In the light of some of the things we have been exploring, hopefully, within the bounds of orthodoxy, it seems fitting to conclude with another quote from St Hilary, this time a call to worship:

> What worthy return can we make for so great a condescension? The One Only-begotten God, ineffably born of God, entered the Virgin's womb and grew and took the frame of poor humanity. He Who upholds the universe, within Whom and through Whom are all things, was brought forth by common childbirth; He at Whose voice Archangels and Angels tremble, and heaven and earth and all the elements of this world are melted, was heard in childish wailing. The Invisible and Incomprehensible, Whom sight and feeling and touch cannot gauge, was wrapped in a cradle ... He by Whom man was made had nothing to gain by becoming Man; it was our gain that God was incarnate and dwelt among us, making all flesh His home by taking upon Him the flesh of One. We were raised because He was lowered; shame to Him was glory to us. He, being God, made flesh His residence,

---

(note 42 *cont.*) these types of temptations. He did not have an inclination towards evil or the "inclination and propensity" of desire towards evil from within. For example, as the Sinless One, filled with the Spirit beyond measure, he did not experience lust in his heart towards a woman; however, that does not mean he did not find certain women attractive. As a man, he would have experienced a natural attraction to a beautiful woman. Beauty is necessarily attractive. Nevertheless, this "attraction" was always kept perfectly in check. Never once did it move to the realm of lust or covetousness.' Pruitt, 'Same Sex Attraction'.

and we in return are lifted anew from the flesh to God.[43]

Questions for reflection and discussion

- How might we balance caution (not rushing in where angels fear to tread) with genuine theological exploration?
- If we are to 'have the same mindset as Christ Jesus' (Phil. 2:5 NIV), what are the implications of Christ's self-emptying for the way we conduct our lives?
- How might we think of the second person of the Trinity being exalted in humility?

Prayer

O heavenly Father, the Author and Fountain of all truth,
The bottomless Sea of all understanding,
Send, we beseech thee,
Thy Holy Spirit into our hearts,
And lighten our understanding with the beams
Of thy heavenly grace.
We ask this, O merciful Father,
For Thy dear Son, our Saviour,
Jesus Christ's sake.
Amen.
(Bishop Nicholas Ridley)

---

43 Hilary of Poitiers, *On the Trinity*, in Philip Schaff, *A Select Library of Nicene and Post-Nicene Fathers of the Christian Church*, Series 2, vol. 9 (New York: Christian Literature Co., 1886–1900), 2.25.

10

God is bigger than we thought

One of the pitfalls when considering the incarnation is to be led astray in our thinking by the kind of language we use. Even allowing for poetic licence in Charles Wesley's 'Let Earth and Heaven Combine' when he writes, 'The incarnate Deity, / Our God *contracted to a span*, / Incomprehensibly made man', it can leave us with the impression that some kind of 'divine downsizing' took place at the incarnation. But as we have been arguing, within the 'Chalcedonian Box' the second person of the Trinity, the eternal Son, did not become man by ceasing to be God; he did not take on human nature at the expense of his divine nature. Divinity did not give way to humanity; rather, it embraced it.

If the eternal Logos, in becoming man, did not cease to be God, then we are not to think, however vaguely, that during the period of the incarnation on earth some sort of 'gap' opened up in the Trinity. If God is omnipresent (everywhere at every time) then even while on earth in the person of Jesus of Nazareth the Logos filled 'all things and was in all places at all times'.[1]

At the time of the Reformation in the sixteenth century during debates concerning the Lord's Supper, this doctrine of what could be thought of as the 'simultaneous presence' of the Son of God in the flesh and in heaven[2] was dubbed by

---

1 Peter Lewis, *The Glory of Christ: Knowing the Man Who Is God* (Chicago: Moody Press, 1997), p. 133.
2 Gerrit Scott Dawson, *Jesus Ascended: The Meaning of Christ's Continuing Incarnation* (Edinburgh: T&T Clark, 2004), pp. 82–89.

Lutherans as the *extra Calvinisticum*, which was a *Schimpfort* (a sneer word) because the '*extra*' was something they claimed the Calvinists had invented. The doctrine is summarized by James Gordon as that which

> states that the eternal Son of God, during his incarnate life on earth, was not enclosed by or limited to the physical body of Jesus Christ but continued to uphold the universe by virtue of maintaining a form of presence beyond or outside of Jesus's body.[3]

Here are John Calvin's own words on the subject, which we referred to earlier:

> For even if the Word in his immeasurable essence united with the nature of man into one person, we do not imagine that he was confined therein. Here is something marvellous: the Son of God descended from heaven in such a way that, without leaving heaven, he willed to be borne in the virgin's womb, to go about the earth, and to hang upon the cross; yet he continuously filled the world even as he had done from the beginning![4]

Helmut Thielicke comments,

> The point of the Calvinistic extra was that Calvin ... did not want to see the second person of the Trinity

---

3   James R. Gordon, 'Holy One in Our Midst: A Dogmatic Defence of the Extra Calvinisticum' (PhD diss., Wheaton College, 2014), p. 1.

4   John Calvin, *Institutes of the Christian Religion*, 2 vols. (ed. John T. McNeill; trans. Ford Lewis Battles; Philadelphia: Westminster, 1960), 1:481.

'exhausted' in the historical man Jesus. The Logos is not completely absorbed by the flesh which He assumes. For He is the subject assuming. He thus transcends it. Consequently He is out of the flesh (*eksarkos*) as well as in it (*ensarkos*).[5]

This is an aspect of the doctrine of the incarnation which is one with Chalcedon and is worth pondering as it provides a wonderful example of where theology (study of God) invariably leads to doxology (worship of God).

A clever invention?

It is openly admitted by scholars that this idea is counter-intuitive[6] but nonetheless it is a doctrine which seeks to ensure that there isn't a separation between the Creator and Ruler from the one who became enfleshed; Jesus is, after all, the one who is 'before all things and in him all things hold together' (Col. 1:17). This 'holding all things together' was not put on hold or delegated during the thirty or so years while Christ was on earth. As Daniel Treier asserts,

> When the Son remains present throughout the universe beyond the human body of Jesus on earth, he is not sneaking around on another project; in the unity of his Spirit with the Father, he continues to participate in divine sustenance of creation and restoration of its proper

---

5 Helmut Thielicke, *The Evangelical Faith*, Vol. 1: *Prolegomena: The Relation of Theology to Modern Thought-Forms* (Grand Rapids: Eerdmans, 1974), pp. 292–293.

6 E.g. Gordon, 'Holy One in Our Midst', p. 266; Daniel J. Treier, 'Incarnation', in Michael Allen and Scott R. Swain (eds.), *Christian Dogmatics: Reformed Theology for the Catholic Church* (Grand Rapids: Baker Academic, 2016), p. 232.

rule. The Son's bringing this rule into our earthly midst reveals the divine benevolence of the redemption in hand.[7]

Far from this being a theological innovation of Calvin's which can be dismissed in a derogatory fashion, it is in fact a wonderful truth to which the Chalcedonian understanding of the person of Christ points. Not surprisingly, throughout the history of the early church there were many prominent theologians who, in their own way, sought to express this mystery of the simultaneous presence of the eternal Word, who was on earth incarnate as the man Jesus Christ whilst also ruling from heaven in perfect union with the Father and the Holy Spirit.

One passage which surfaces time and time again and which provided the biblical mine from which this theological gold could be retrieved is John 3 and Jesus' conversation with Nicodemus.

Not so new

John Chrysostom (349–407)

We begin with the giant of the East, John Chrysostom.

The paradox of Christ being in heaven while also being on earth is observed in Jesus' encounter with Nicodemus, and so Chrysostom writes,

Touching him [Nicodemus] therefore very severely, Christ goes on to show that He knoweth not these things

---

7   Treier, 'Incarnation', pp. 232–233.

only, but others also, far more and greater than these. And this He declared by what follows, when He said, 'And no man hath ascended up to heaven, but He that came down from heaven, even the Son of Man which *is* in heaven.' . . . Seest thou how even that which appears very exalted is utterly unworthy of His greatness? *For not in heaven only is He, but everywhere, and He fills all things;* but yet He speaks according to the infirmity of His hearer, desiring to lead him up little by little. And in this place He called not the flesh 'Son of Man', but He now names, so to speak, His entire Self from the inferior substance; indeed this is His wont, to call His whole Person often from His Divinity, and often from His humanity.[8]

Chrysostom takes what Jesus says quite literally when he speaks of the Son of Man 'which *is* in heaven' while Jesus is on earth speaking these words. He makes his belief in the omnipresence of the Son plain by saying that he is 'everywhere and He fills all things', echoing the kind of language we find Paul using in Ephesians 1:23. This is hardly any different from what Calvin was to write centuries later: that while on earth as God incarnate, the Son was also in heaven fulfilling his relationship with the Father and the Spirit in being Sustainer of all creation – being the one who 'sustains all things by the power of his word' (my translation). The Son didn't cease fulfilling this divine role while he was walking by the shores of Galilee as a man.

---

8 John Chrysostom, Homily 27, *Homilies on the Gospel According to St John*, in Philip Schaff, *A Select Library of Nicene and Post-Nicene Fathers of the Christian Church*, Series 1, vol. 14 (New York: Christian Literature Co., 1886–1900); emphasis added.

Augustine (354–430)

If Chrysostom was the undisputed theological giant of the East, Augustine of Hippo was the towering colossus of the West.

Referring to the same passage as Chrysostom – John 3 – we find Augustine writing in similar vein,

> He [Jesus] says, 'No man has ascended into heaven but He that came down from heaven, the Son of Man who is in heaven.' He said not 'was' but, saith He, 'the Son of Man who is in heaven'. He was speaking on earth, and He declares Himself to be in heaven. And yet He did not speak thus: 'No man hath ascended into heaven but He that came down from heaven,' the Son of God 'who is in heaven'. Whither tends it but to make us understand that . . . Christ both God and man, is one person, not two persons . . . Christ, therefore is one . . . *In heaven He was when He spoke on earth.* He was Son of Man in heaven in that manner in which He was Son of God on earth; Son of God on earth in the flesh which He took, Son of Man in heaven in the unity of person.[9]

Because of the unity of his human nature with the Divine, and because of his unbroken unity with his Father in heaven, it is possible to say that Jesus could be understood to be the Son of Man *in* heaven *while* incarnate on earth.

This was no isolated theme for Augustine, either. Still in John's Gospel, this time chapter 2, Augustine wrote of the Son,

---

9 Augustine, *Tractates on John*, in Schaff, *Nicene and Post-Nicene Fathers*, Series 1, vol. 7 (Edinburgh: T&T Clark; Grand Rapids: Eerdmans, 1993), 12:8; emphasis added.

He *departed not from the Father; and came to us.* He sucked the breasts, and He contained the world. He lay in the manger, and He fed the Angels. God and Man, the same God who is Man, the same Man who is God. But not God in that wherein He is Man, God, in that He is the Word; *Man in that the Word was made flesh; by at once continuing to be God,* assuming Man's Flesh; by adding what He was not, not losing what He was.[10]

Notice how finely balanced and careful Augustine is in what he says. He speaks of the 'feeding of angels' while Christ lay in a manger, and yet speaks of this action as not being of 'God in that wherein He is Man' but of 'God, in that He is the Word'. And so he cannot be accused of suggesting 'the monstrosity of the baby Jesus lying in the manger possessing full divine consciousness' of which Craig spoke, for there is no suggestion that the baby Jesus had any 'divine consciousness' by which such divine activity could take place. Rather, it was as the eternal *Word* who *at the same time* was incarnate as the babe in Bethlehem that the cosmic Lordship of Christ continued to be exercised.

The paradox that the eternal Word did 'not leave the Father' when 'He came to us' is held by Augustine without any embarrassment or hint of apology. The incarnation within the 'Chalcedonian Box' would seem to suggest, if not demand, that the Logos, in taking to himself full humanity, did not in any way diminish his divinity, and that includes the attributes of omnipresence and omniscience.

---

10 Augustine, *Sermons on Selected Lessons*, 73.3, in *Tractates on John*, emphasis added.

If we think Augustine is waxing eloquent in that passage, he simply surpasses himself in this next one:

> He so loved us that for our sake He was made man in time, through Whom all times were made; was in the world less in years than His servants, though older than the world itself in His eternity; was made man, Who made man; was created of a mother, whom He created; was carried by hands which He formed; nursed at the breasts which He had filled; cried in the manger in word-less infancy, He the Word without Whom all human eloquence is mute.[11]

It could be argued that these are the logical entailments of the doctrine of the person of Christ as forged in the great ecumenical creeds. They certainly defy the imagination and stretch human language to the limit, but surely they do call forth from us some attempt to express, if not in theological language which is neat and tidy, the heart of our belief that God became man without ceasing to be God.

Hilary of Poitiers (310–367)

A few years earlier, Hilary had anticipated Augustine on this issue. We saw in the last chapter how Hilary warned against the dangers of incautious speculation concerning divine mysteries, but nonetheless on this matter he felt compelled to discuss the difficulty of how Christ could remain in heaven and descend to earth. As with Chrysostom and Augustine such

---

11 Augustine, Sermon 188, *Sermons on Selected Lessons of the New Testament*, in Schaff, *Nicene and Post-Nicene Fathers*, Series 1, vol. 6 (Edinburgh: T&T Clark; Grand Rapids: Eerdmans, 1993).

musings arose out of a study of Scripture, and, again like Chrysostom and Augustine, it was John's Gospel and especially chapter 3 which provided the catalyst for such thinking:

> For the present I will speak of the Incarnation only. Tell me, I pray, you who pry into secrets of Heaven, the mystery of Christ born of a Virgin and His nature; whence will you explain that He was conceived and born of a Virgin? What was the physical cause of His origin according to your disputations? How was He formed within His mother's womb? Whence His body and His humanity? And lastly, what does it mean that the *Son of Man descended from heaven Who remained in heaven*, John 3:13? It is not possible by the laws of bodies for the same object to remain and to descend: the one is the change of downward motion; the other the stillness of being at rest. *The Infant wails but is in Heaven: the Boy grows but remains ever the immeasurable God.* By what perception of human understanding can we comprehend that *He ascended where He was before, and He descended Who remained in heaven*? The Lord says, 'What if you should behold the Son of Man ascending there where He was before?' The Son of Man ascends where He was before: can sense apprehend this? *The Son of Man descends from heaven, Who is in heaven*: can reason cope with this? The Word was made flesh: can words express this? The Word becomes flesh, that is, God becomes Man: the Man is in heaven: the God is from heaven. He ascends Who descended: but *He descends and yet does not descend.* He is as He ever was, yet He was not ever what He is. We pass in review the causes, but we cannot explain the manner:

we perceive the manner, and we cannot understand the causes. Yet if we understand Christ Jesus even thus, we shall know Him: if we seek to understand Him further we shall not know Him at all.[12]

Hilary does not hold back from piling paradox upon paradox in order to do justice to the Chalcedonian understanding of Christ. The Son of Man ascends to where he was 'before' and yet he descended while 'remaining in heaven'. He 'descends' and yet 'does not descend'. The infant in the manger cries and yet 'is in Heaven' (not the baby of flesh but the Word who *at the same time* is united to the baby enhypostatically). As Gerrit Dawson concludes, 'Such moving and remaining, remaining and moving can only be understood in terms of the one to which the actions point: the one Christ in two natures.'[13]

Ephraim the Semite (d. 373)

Whilst not having the same theological acumen as a Chrysostom or an Augustine, this fourth-century Middle Eastern mystic is worth referring to, not least because his writings show that the 'extra' of Calvin is not 'extra' at all but a widely held belief however tentatively grasped or loosely formulated. If we think Augustine's theology was poetry, Ephraim's can be considered Poet Laureate material!

The High One became as a little child, and in Him was hidden a treasure of wisdom sufficing for all! Though

---

12 Hilary of Poitiers, *On the Trinity*, in Schaff, *Nicene and Post-Nicene Fathers*, Series 2, vol. 9 (New York: Christian Literature Co., 1886–1900), 10.54; emphasis added.
13 Gerrit Scott Dawson, *Jesus Ascended: The Meaning of Christ's Continuing Incarnation* (Edinburgh: T&T Clark, 2004), p. 87.

Most High, yet He sucked the milk of Mary, and of His goodness all creatures suck ... While He was lying on His mother's bosom, in His bosom were all creatures lying. He was silent as a babe, and yet He was making creatures execute all His commands. For without the First-born no man can approach unto the essence, to which He is equal. The thirty years He was in the earth, Who was ordering all creatures, Who was receiving offerings of praise from those above and those below. He was wholly in the depths and wholly in the highest! He was wholly with all things and wholly with each. While His body was forming within the womb, His power was fashioning all members! While the Conception of the Son was fashioning the womb, He Himself was fashioning babes in the womb!

Ephraim then moves on from contemplating the birth of Christ to pondering his death, with his thoughts being framed by the 'simultaneous presence' of the Son:

For see how, when He was wholly hanging upon the Cross, His Power was yet making all creatures move! For He darkened the sun and made the earth quake; He rent the graves and brought forth the dead! See how when He was wholly on the Cross, yet again He was wholly everywhere.[14]

It might be argued that much of what Ephraim wrote arose out of intuition rather than being the result of deep theological reflection, but even so, surely the intuitions are right. According

14 Ephraim the Syrian, Hymn 3, *Nineteen Hymns on the Nativity of Christ in the Flesh*, in Schaff, *Nicene and Post-Nicene Fathers*, Series 2, vol. 13 (New York: Christian Literature Co., 1886–1900).

to the psalmist, it was the Lord who knitted him together in his mother's womb (Ps. 139), and if that is so, then the Son who is Lord and Creator was fashioning babies in *their* mothers' wombs even as he was developing within the womb of Mary – which may lie behind what Ephraim is eulogizing. And even at the point of Jesus' greatest weakness, physically and mentally at Calvary, the Son was still exercising his creational power. It follows that it was by his divine say-so that the atoms of the nails which held him to the cross continued to be.

Athanasius (296–373)

Even earlier than any of these writers, we find the scourge of the Arians, Athanasius, writing in terms not wholly dissimilar. In his famous treatise on the incarnation we find this description of the incarnate Christ:

> The Word was not hedged in by His body, nor did His presence in the body prevent His being present elsewhere as well . . . At one and the same time – this is the wonder – as Man He was living a human life, and as Word He was sustaining the life of the Universe, and as Son He was in constant union with the Father.[15]

Calvin speaks of the Word not being 'confined'; Athanasius, of the Word not being 'hedged in'. Calvin refers to the Word 'continuously filling the world'; Athanasius, as 'being present elsewhere as well'. Both inhabit the same theological world of ideas which flow from the orthodox view of the person of

---

15 Athanasius, *On the Incarnation of the Word* 3.17, in *On the Incarnation: St Athanasius, with an Introduction by C. S. Lewis* (Crestwood, NY: St Vladimir's Seminary Press, 1998), p. 45.

Christ, with Athanasius anticipating Chalcedon and Calvin looking back to it.

Thomas Aquinas (1225–1274)

The final theologian we will look at who held to these same ideas, thus showing that Calvin was certainly not going out on a theological limb, is another theological giant, the medieval monk Thomas Aquinas:

> Not even in the hypostatic union is the Word of God or the divine nature comprehended by the human nature. Although the divine nature was wholly united to the human nature in the one Person of the Son, nevertheless the whole power of the divinity was not, as it were, circumscribed.[16]

For Calvin, the Word was not 'confined'; for Athanasius, the Word was not 'hedged in'; and similarly for Aquinas, the Word was not 'circumscribed'. To justify his position, Aquinas quotes from one of Augustine's letters which was also used by Calvin in his own defence:

> I would have you know that it is not Christian doctrine that God was so poured into the flesh in which he was born of the Virgin that he either abandoned or lost care of the government of the universe or that he transferred this care into that small body as into a gathered and contracted material.[17]

---

16 Thomas Aquinas, *Summa Theologica* 3.10.1.2.
17 Augustine, *Letter 137 to Volusian*, in Edward T. Oakes, *Infinity Dwindled to Infancy: A Catholic and Evangelical Christology* (Grand Rapids: Eerdmans, 2011), p. 267.

Comprehending and apprehending

A number of years ago I visited the Grand Canyon. Standing on the rim and looking down into the giant gorge and the fast-flowing Colorado River, I had an experience which was not uncommon: namely, feeling vertiginous, dizzy. The depths were too great to contemplate and remain steady; after all, it is not called the *Grand* Canyon for nothing! That may have been your feeling too as we surveyed the writings of some of the greatest theologians of previous centuries as they considered how the one who was and always will be the eternal Logos, God the Son, could become a genuine human being who, at one level, was subject to all the limitations and vagaries of space and time and yet continued operating, as it were, beyond space and time.

Sometimes theologians are accused of hiding behind the idea of a 'mystery' when they come to the limits of their comprehension. But such an accusation can be misplaced. There does come a point in any discipline where limits are reached and are to be acknowledged. This is not a cop-out, it is simply an honest 'owning up'. This brings us to an important and helpful distinction as we think on the incarnation: the difference between comprehending and apprehending.[18]

In discussing the mysteries regarding the person of Christ, the Puritan John Owen remarked, 'What we shall farther comprehend of them in the other world, God only knows.'[19] The incarnation is truly beyond human comprehension, but nonetheless we can *apprehend* some aspects of it, gaining a real,

---

18 See Paul Helm, 'The Mystery of the Incarnation: "Great Is the Mystery of Godliness"', *The Southern Baptist Journal of Theology* 19.1 (2015), pp. 25–37.
19 Cited by Helm, 'Mystery of the Incarnation', p. 26.

though partial understanding. Hopefully, this chapter has helped us 'apprehend', seeing into a glass, however dimly, and in so doing marvelling all the more at the God who became man without ceasing to be God.

Questions for reflection and discussion

- A number of years ago, the Bible translator J. B. Phillips wrote a book entitled *Your God Is Too Small*. How does this chapter enlarge your vision of God in Christ?
- Whilst not comprehending how God the Son could 'remain in heaven whilst descending from heaven', what have you apprehended?
- What difference will this have on your approach to the worship of Jesus?

Prayer

Late have I loved thee, O thou Eternal Truth and Goodness,
Late have I sought thee, my Father!
But thou didst seek me, and when thou shinest forth upon me,
Then I knew thee and learnt to love thee.
I thank thee, O my light,
That thou didst shine upon me;
That thou didst teach me my soul
What thou wouldst be to me,
And didst incline thy face in pity upon me.
Thou, Lord, hast become my hope, my comfort,
My strength, my all.
In thee doth my soul rejoice.
Amen.
(Augustine of Hippo)

11

Why it matters

When engaging in any study, whether it is in the area of science, literature, history, politics or theology, three questions are worth asking: 'What?', 'So what?' and 'Now what?'

For most of the second section of this book, we have mainly been focusing on the first question: '*What* is the incarnation?' We have seen that the consensus of the church has been that in order to do justice to the inspired biblical testimony, Christians affirm that Jesus Christ is both divine and human united in one person. In taking to himself full humanity, the second person of the Trinity remained fully God. There was no divine subtraction in the divine self-emptying, but a human addition: God being united with human flesh for all eternity.

Inevitably we have wandered into thinking about the second question, 'So what?' Here we have seen that God the Son came into time so that united to him by faith we might go to be with him in eternity. That is a very big 'So what?'! But there are many more implications, both doctrinal and practical. In this final chapter we are going to draw things together by thinking a little further on the last two questions, not least the 'Now what?'

The centrality of the incarnation

C. S. Lewis wrote to Arthur Greaves on 11 December 1941, 'The doctrine of Christ's divinity seems to me not something stuck on which you can unstick but something that peeps out at every point so that you'd have to unravel the whole web to get rid of it.'[1] He was right.

Lewis speaks of a 'web' which would have to be 'unravelled' in order to remove the doctrine. Interestingly enough, it was the philosopher W. V. O. Quine who defined a belief as 'a complicated, interconnected web of ideas'.[2] We can think of a person's belief as being like a spider's web. Some elements of the belief will lie close to the edge of the web, having a more direct impact on day-to-day living. Others will be located more towards the interior of the web, being essential for holding the rest of the web together, giving it coherence and strength. Although some of these elements of belief may *seem* a little abstract, they are a core part of a global set of beliefs about what we consider reality to be. Theology, strictly speaking, is concerned with *reality in Jesus Christ*.[3] As such, the incarnation – who Jesus is – lies at the centre of that web of beliefs called the Christian faith. Any attempt to remove it or reduce it will result in a truncated version of Christianity at best or an altogether different religion at worst. Belief in the incarnation is, in the words of Lewis, not simply 'stuck on'. Going to the heart of the matter as usual, Dorothy L. Sayers wrote, 'If Christ was only man, then he is entirely irrelevant to any thought about God; if he is only God, then he is entirely irrelevant to any experience in human life.'[4] Christ is both God and man and so the word 'relevance' seems almost too weak to describe

1   Cited in Alister McGrath, *Studies in Doctrine* (Grand Rapids: Zondervan, 1997), p. 329.
2   W. V. O. Quine, *From a Logical Point of View* (2nd rev. edn; New York: Scribner's, 1967), pp. 42–44.
3   Kevin J. Vanhoozer, *The Pastor as Public Theologian: Reclaiming a Lost Vision* (Grand Rapids: Baker, 2015), p. 110.
4   Cited in Alister E. McGrath, *Understanding Doctrine* (London: Hodder & Stoughton, 1990), p. 329.

his significance in relation to our thoughts about God and human life.

Requiring an explanation

From a purely cultural and historical point of view the significance of Jesus cannot be overestimated.

A number of years ago the celebrated Harvard historian Jaroslav Pelikan wrote:

> Regardless of what anyone may personally think or believe about him, Jesus of Nazareth has been the dominant figure in the history of Western culture for almost twenty centuries. If it were possible, with some sort of super magnet, to pull out of that history every scrap of metal bearing at least a trace of his name, how much would be left?[5]

The answer is: not very much. Even our calendar reflects his coming, distinguishing AD from BC. From a purely human point of view his monumental and irreversible impact on the world is very difficult, if not impossible, to account for.

In his own lifetime he was highly dismissive of the power and glory merchants of his day, so he held no high office of influence. Given his homeless lifestyle, today he would be harassed and moved on by the police if he lived in Europe. Given his teenage mother's lack of a wedding ring, he would have been an automatic candidate for abortion if conceived in Britain. Given his ancestry, had he lived in Germany in the 1930s he, in all likelihood, would have been pinned with a

---

5   Jaroslav Pelikan, *Jesus Through the Centuries* (New York: Harper & Row, 1987), p. 1.

yellow star and shipped to a death camp. He never wrote a book, his public ministry lasted less than three years and at the end of it all he was deserted by his closest friends, and yet today there are millions and millions of people all around the world who literally worship him. These things need some explanation. That explanation, at least in part, is given by the Chalcedonian Creed: Jesus is God who became man.

Three mysteries

We noted earlier Fred Sanders' claim that whilst Christian truth is made up of a great many doctrines, there are only three great mysteries which are to be found at the heart of Christianity, at the centre of the theological web of beliefs: the incarnation, the Trinity and the atonement.[6] The incarnation is intimately interrelated to both other doctrines as we shall see, further underscoring its importance.

True divinity

Since Jesus is the exact representation of God (Heb. 1:3), in him we have a genuine revelation of God. 'Anyone who has seen me has seen the Father' (John 14:9 NIV), Jesus told his disciples. This doesn't mean that Jesus *is* the Father in the guise of a Son (the heresy of modalism), nor that he is wholly detached from the Father so that he is a revelation of only one 'aspect' of God. The reason why in 'seeing' Jesus we 'see' the Father is because of what Jesus went on to say next:

---

6 Fred Sanders, 'Chalcedonian Categories for the Gospel Narrative', in Fred Sanders and Klaus Issler (eds.), *Jesus in Trinitarian Perspective: An Introductory Christology* (Nashville: Broadman & Holman, 2007), pp. 1–43 [8].

Don't you believe that I am *in* the Father, and that the Father is *in* me? The words I say to you I do not speak on my own authority. Rather, it is the Father, living *in* me, who is doing his work. Believe me when I say that I am *in* the Father and the Father is *in* me.

(John 14:10–11 NIV)

The idea here is of 'mutual indwelling'.

This passage in John's Gospel reveals the special and intimate nature of the relationship between the Father and the Son such that to encounter the one is simultaneously to encounter the other. If you are in the presence of the Son you are *also* in the presence of the Father, for the Son *mediates* his presence. (This idea was particularly developed by the Cappadocian theologians as captured by the famous saying of Gregory of Nazianzus, 'No sooner do I conceive of the one than I am illumined by the splendour of the three; no sooner do I distinguish them than I am carried back to the one.')[7] Therefore, we are not to think of Father and Son as two individuals who have an existence independent of each other. Rather, their identity (who they are) arises out of their relationship to each other. God the Father is Father by virtue of the fact that he eternally begets the Son. The Son is Son by virtue of the fact that he is eternally begotten of the Father. And yet they remain distinct persons, for you need at least 'two centres of consciousness' to love: a lover and a beloved.[8] This mutual indwelling

---

7 Cited by Robert Letham, 'The Trinity in Worship', in Brandon D. Crowe and Carl R. Trueman (eds.), *The Essential Trinity* (London: Apollos, 2016), p. 269.

8 J. Scott Horrell defines a person as 'a centre of self-consciousness existing in relationship to others'. J. Scott Horrell, 'The Eternal Son of God in the Social Trinity', in Sanders and Issler, *Jesus in Trinitarian Perspective*, pp. 44–79 [52]. In the same volume, Garrett J. DeWeese defines a person as 'an individual with appropriately complex and structured mental properties, faculties (a natural grouping of capacities) and higher

which ensures the unity of the Godhead whilst respecting the distinctiveness of persons has been given a name by the Eastern Church theologians (going back to John of Damascus in the eighth century): *perichoresis*. The theologian Miroslav Volf describes it as 'co-inherence in one another without any coalescence or commixture'.[9]

The Holy Spirit, it is argued, is the *perichoresis* of the Father and the Son. Tom Smail describes it in this way:

> The 'fellowship of the Holy Spirit' (2 Cor. 13:14) revealed in God's relating to us reflects that 'fellowship' within the life of God ... The Spirit can be seen as the person who mediates, sustains and enables the love between the Father and the Son, so that by his personal action he both unites them in an inexpressibly close way but at the same time constitutes himself as 'the space' between them so that they do not collapse into each other but remain in their distinct personal integrity over against each other.

He goes on,

> This is what we see happening in the baptism of Jesus, where the Father gives himself to the Son in giving him his Spirit and remains distinct from the incarnate Son in his heavenly glory. He is thus the Spirit who, by simultaneously relating and maintaining the distinct personhood

---

(note 8 *cont.*) order capacities, unified by internal relations', which is a re-presentation of Boethius.' Garrett J. DeWeese, 'One Person, Two Natures: Two Metaphysical Models of the Incarnation', in Sanders and Issler, *Jesus in Trinitarian Perspective*, pp. 114–155 [138].

9 Miroslav Volf, *After Our Likeness: The Church as the Image of the Trinity* (Grand Rapids: Eerdmans, 1998), p. 209.

of the other two, is not reduced to a relationship but is to be seen as the person who completes and unites the godhead in his relating of the Father to the Son.[10]

In Christ we know God truly; we apprehend, although do not fully comprehend, God.

Professor Mackintosh's almost doxological response to this amazing truth captures well what should be the response of every Christian: 'When I look into the face of Jesus Christ and see the face of God, I know that I have not seen that face else-where, for he and the Father are one.'[11] He then makes this very important point:

> we must see him at the centre of all things. We must behold him as the pivotal and cardinal reality, round which all life and history have moved. That is a place out of which his Person cannot be kept.[12]

And yet the pressure today is to relativize Christ, to see him as *one* way to God but not *the* way, to consider him to be *a* face but not *the* face of God. In our world of increased pluralization this pressure has become more acute; there-fore a strong and uncompromising belief in the incarnation which guarantees the uniqueness and exclusivity of Christ is *all the more* crucial if the pressure is to be resisted and the church is not to inadvertently drift into a new kind of Unitarianism.

---

10 Tom Smail, *Like Father, Like Son: The Trinity Imaged in Our Humanity* (Carlisle: Paternoster, 2005), p. 100.
11 H. R. Mackintosh, *The Person of Jesus Christ* (ed. T. F. Torrance; Edinburgh: T&T Clark, 2007), p. 77.
12 Mackintosh, *The Person of Jesus Christ*, p. 50.

The jealousy that Christians should instinctively feel towards any relativization of Christ was movingly illustrated by Henry Martyn.

In 1805 Martyn left England for India and later moved to Iran in order to engage in missionary work there. Martyn was a first-class scholar at Cambridge University. He translated the New Testament into Hindi and Persian so that Muslims who spoke those languages could hear the gospel. His Christian devotion was so intense and his love for Christ was so deep that he could hardly bear the thought of any disgrace being brought to the name of Christ. In Shiraz, a year before his death at the age of thirty-one, somebody said in his presence that the crown prince of Persia had killed so many Russian Christians in battle that 'Christ had taken hold of Mohammed's skirt and begged him to stop'. Henry Martyn wrote in his journal, 'I was cut to the soul at this blasphemy. I could not endure existence if Jesus were not glorified; it would be hell to me, if he were to be always thus dishonoured.'[13] Here was someone who knew in his *heart* the supreme revelation of God in Christ which would tolerate no rivals.

Making too much of the incarnation in the wrong way

As far back as 1889, with the publication of a series of essays by Anglo-Catholic theologians entitled *Lux Mundi*, the notion of Christ's self-giving in his self-humbling was taken and applied to the church as 'the body of Christ'. This led to the notion that the *church* itself can be thought of as an *extension of the*

---

13 Cited by John R. W. Stott, *Life in Christ* (London: Candle Books, 1991), p. 91.

incarnation. Sometimes this idea is expressed at the level of popular piety in the way captured by the teaching of the sixteenth-century Catholic mystic Teresa of Ávila:

> Christ has no body now, but yours.
> No hands, no feet on earth, but yours.
> Yours are the eyes through which
> Christ looks compassion into the world.
> Yours are the feet
> with which Christ walks to do good.
> Yours are the hands
> with which Christ blesses all the world.[14]

At the level of basic theology, this is, of course, nonsense. Christ *does* have a body: it is in heaven as he reigns in and through that body at the right hand of the Father. This is an example of taking a biblical truth – in this case, that we are the body of Christ (1 Cor. 12:27) – and extending its significance in a direction which was never intended. It stretches the metaphor to breaking point and effectively destroys it.

In 1988, the then Archbishop of Canterbury, Robert Runcie, chided a gathering of Anglican evangelicals for not having given much thought to the subject of 'ecclesiology', the doctrine of the church. He said, 'If it [the Church] is the Body of Christ, the Church too demands our belief, trust and faith.'[15] Such a statement betrays a view echoing the papal encyclical of 1943 *Mystici corporis Christi*, which goes beyond Scripture to the point of identifying and confusing the church *with* Christ by a misappropriation of the analogy of 'the body'. In fact, it borders

---

14 Order of the Carmelites https://ocarm.org/en/content/ocarm/teresa-avila-quotes.
15 In Melvin Tinker, 'N.E.A.C. 3: A Conference Too Far?', *Churchman* 102.4 (1988), p. 318.

on the blasphemous by urging a loyalty to the church which should be reserved for Christ alone.[16]

As John Webster writes, 'Any extension of the incarnation . . . can be Christologically disastrous, in that it may threaten the uniqueness of the Word's becoming flesh by making "incarnation" a general principle or characteristic of divine action in, through, or under creaturely reality.'[17] Such talk of the Christian's 'incarnating' God's presence or 'incarnating the gospel', which is becoming increasingly common even within evangelical circles, actually devalues the incarnation, robbing it of its uniqueness and significance. This must firmly be resisted.

What is at stake?

What is at stake in holding to the orthodox understanding of the relationship between the Trinity, incarnation and the atonement has been helpfully summarized by Peter Adam:

> Without the doctrine of the Trinity it would be ridiculous to claim that we know the heart of God, for 'no-one has ever seen God. It is only God the Son, who is close to the Father's heart, who has made him known' (John 1:18). We could not claim that Jesus is the way, the truth and the life, for no-one comes to the Father except through him (John 14:6). We could not rightly address Jesus as 'My Lord and my God' (John 20:28). We could not affirm that

16 See Tinker, 'N.E.A.C. 3', pp. 316–324.
17 John Webster, *Holy Scripture: A Dogmatic Sketch* (Cambridge: Cambridge University Press, 2003), pp. 22–23.

'there is salvation in no-one else, for there is no other name under heaven given among mortals by which we must be saved' (Acts 4:12). We could not assert that 'in Christ God was reconciling the world to himself . . . for our sake, he made him to be sin who knew no sin, so that in him we might become the righteousness of God' (2 Cor. 5:19, 21). We could not look forward to the day when 'at the name of Jesus every knee shall bow and every tongue confess that Jesus Christ is Lord, to the glory of God the Father' (Phil. 2:10–11). Finally, we could not anticipate the great song of Revelation 5: 'You are worthy to take the scroll and to open its seals, for you were slaughtered and by your blood you ransomed for God saints from every tribe and language and people and nation' (Rev. 5:9).

He concludes,

> We can only rightly honour Jesus Christ as the only Son of the Father, as the one who has made God known, as the only Saviour and Mediator, if we have the essential truths of the doctrine of the Trinity as our foundation.[18]

True humanity

In Christ we have a genuine revelation of what God is like, the true identity and character of God. But we are also given a revelation of what true humanity is like. Michael Reeves describes this 'double revelation' in the following way:

---

18 Peter Adam, 'Honouring Jesus Christ', *Churchman* 119.1 (Spring 2005), <https://biblicalstudies.org.uk/pdf/churchman/119-01_035.pdf>.

The eternal Son of God has always been characterized by such love, such purity and vivaciousness. Now he has brought that life to us, to be the firstborn of the new humanity, and this is how humanity complete in him looks. Here in the Son of Man is both the *identity* and the *character* of the new humanity.[19]

There is a theological 'golden chain' which links Christ's taking on human nature, carrying out atonement and our new humanity in him.

The impression can be given in some quarters of the church that the incarnation itself saves us. That is not the case. It is a *necessary* condition ('what is not assumed is not healed') but not a *sufficient* condition, for sin has to be dealt with and reconciliation between God and ourselves brought about:

Since therefore the children share in flesh and blood, he himself likewise partook of the same things, that through death he might destroy the one who has the power of death, that is, the devil, and deliver all those who through fear of death were subject to lifelong slavery . . . Therefore he had to be made like his brothers in every respect, so that he might become a merciful and faithful high priest in the service of God, to make propitiation for the sins of the people. (Heb. 2:14–17)

The inseparable link between the incarnation, the atonement and our union in Christ has been expressed by Robert Letham in these terms:

---

19 Michael Reeves, *Rejoicing in Christ* (Downers Grove: InterVarsity Press, 2015), p. 54.

In itself, the incarnation of the Son of God does not unite us to him, for by itself it does not accomplish salvation. Christ united himself to a human nature, not the nature of the elect . . . There is no incarnation without atonement.

That much is clear. He then goes on:

On the other hand, there is no atonement without incarnation . . . It was in our nature that he offered himself to the Father on the cross, and in our nature that he ascended far above all things created, and in our nature that he lives and reigns forever – in indissoluble personal union. Therefore, the incarnation is more than the basis for this union, as though the union were something else, separable and inherently disconnected. The complete identification of the eternal Son with our flesh and blood is part of our union with him . . . So the incarnation should not be seen as merely a means to salvation. Rather, salvation finds its ultimate fulfilment in the union of humanity with God seen in the incarnate Christ. If, from one angle, the incarnation was the means of atonement and all that followed it, from another (more lasting) perspective, the atonement was the means to the elevation and fruition of humanity in the renewed cosmos over which Christ rules, and we in him.[20]

Letham shows how the three mysteries spoken of by Fred Sanders forming the core of Christian belief can be thought of in terms of three *unions*:

---

20 Robert Letham, *Union with Christ: In Scripture, History, and Theology* (Phillipsburg: P&R, 2011), pp. 40–41.

The Christian faith can be summed up as, *inter alia*, a series of unions. There is the union of the three persons in the Trinity, the union of the Son of God with our human nature, the union of Christ with his church, the union established by the Holy Spirit with us as he indwells us.[21]

Working it out

Let's think more specifically about the 'Now what?'

Because of Christ taking on human nature and atoning for our sins, and believers being united to him by faith, we share his status as sons and we become his brothers:

> For it was fitting that he, for whom and by whom all things exist, in bringing many sons to glory, should make the founder of their salvation perfect through suffering. For he who sanctifies and those who are sanctified all have one source. That is why he is not ashamed to call them brothers. (Heb. 2:10–11)

This has tremendous pastoral implications.

The first is for *when Christians fall into sin*. In his deeply moving exposition of Christ's high priestly office in Hebrews,[22] the Puritan Thomas Goodwin shows how Jesus empathizes with us far more than does even the closest friend:

> Your very sins move him to pity more than anger . . . it is true, his pity increased all the more towards you, just like

---

21 Letham, *Union with Christ*, p. 37.
22 Thomas Goodwin, *The Works of Thomas Goodwin* (Edinburgh: James Nichols, 1862), 4:149.

the heart of a father to a child that has some terrible disease . . . his hatred shall fall only upon the sin, to free you from its ruin and destruction, his very compassion is drawn out more and more to you and this is as much as when you fall under the influence of sin as under any other affliction. Therefore, don't be afraid, 'What shall separate us from Christ's love.'

Commenting on this passage, Michael Reeves writes,

His point is that those who are in Christ have a new identity, defined by Christ and not by sin. Sin in the believer is a sickness, a sickness he hates, but which draws out his compassion. In glory, Jesus' first reaction when you sin is pity. Where you would run *from* him in guilt, he would run *to* you in grace. It makes all the difference when your heart feels cold and cloddish. Right then you can know that your weary joylessness fills *him* with compassion.[23]

Having become one of us, Jesus is able to sympathize with us.

The second implication is for *when we suffer*. Knowing that God has become one of us and has suffered for us, having walked through this vale of tears, makes all the difference in the world in enabling Christians to cope with the problem of pain. Let me give one example.

Baroness Caroline Cox, former deputy speaker of the House of Lords, has been described as 'the Mother Teresa of the war-torn poor'. As a former nurse, she personally supervises

---

23 Michael Reeves, *Rejoicing in Christ* (Downers Grove: InterVarsity Press, 2015), p. 76.

Christian relief to many of the war-ravaged areas of the world, actually going to the front line to help with the distribution of food, clothes and medicine. Often when she arrives people greet her with these words: 'Thank God you've come. We thought the world had forgotten us.'

Once she was asked to relate both her worst and her best moments during all her journeys of mercy.[24] The worst? She thought for a moment and then described what it was like to enter a Dinka village after the Sudanese government-backed soldiers had left. The stench of death, she said, was simply overpowering. More than a hundred corpses lay where they had been butchered. Men, women, children, even cattle, had been cut down or people had been herded into captivity as slaves. Straw huts were set ablaze; devastation and death affronted eyes everywhere. Worst of all was the knowledge that the militia would return. 'Genocide is an overworked word,' Baroness Cox said, 'and one I would never use without meaning it. But I mean it.'

What of her best moment? This, she said, came straight after the worst. With the raiders gone and the results of their cruelty all around – husbands slain, children kidnapped into slavery, homes ruined, the women brutally raped – the few women still alive were pulling themselves together. Their first instinctive act was to make tiny crosses out of sticks lying on the ground and to push them into the earth.

What were they doing? Baroness Cox explained that the crudely formed crosses were not markers of death, but symbols of hope. The crossed sticks, pressed into the ground at the moment when their world had all but been destroyed, were acts

---

24 In Os Guinness, *Unspeakable: Facing Up to Evil in an Age of Genocide and Terror* (San Francisco: HarperSanFrancisco, 2005), pp. 136–137.

of faith. As followers of the Lord Jesus Christ, they served a God who they believed knew pain as they knew pain. Blinded by pain and grief themselves, frighteningly aware that the world would neither know nor care about their plight, they staked their lives on the conviction that there was one who knew 'from the inside' and who cared, and that they were not alone. The incarnation was no abstract belief for these people, nor is it for many Christians suffering throughout the world; it is *the* anchor which holds their faith firm in the midst of the wildfire storms of life.

The third implication is that the incarnation *is crucial to our apologetics.*

Here we see the difference Christianity makes compared with all other beliefs. In contrast to secular humanism which views suffering as, in the words of Richard Dawkins, just 'damn bad luck', necessary for the evolutionary process; or to Theravada Buddhism, which considers suffering to be the result of desire which binds us to the wheel of *samsara* and the process of reincarnation until we are eventually released to become nothing – *nirvana* – Christianity recognizes that the world could have been otherwise but for human sin, and that God has taken steps to do something about it by coming into the world as a man who went to the cross.

John Stott, reflecting on this truth of the 'suffering God', wrote:

I could never believe in God, if it were not for the cross. The only God I believe in is the one Nietzsche ridiculed as 'God on the cross'. In the real world of pain, how could one worship a God who was immune from it? I have entered many Buddhist temples in different Asian countries and stood respectfully before the statue of the Buddha, his legs crossed, arms folded, eyes closed, the ghost of a smile playing round his mouth, a remote look on his face, detached from the agonies of the world. But each time after a while I have turned away, and in my imagination I have turned instead to that lonely, twisted, tortured figure on the cross, nails through hands and feet, back lacerated, limbs wrenched, brow bleeding from thorn pricks, mouth dry and intolerably thirsty, plunged in God-forsaken darkness. That is the God for me! He laid aside immunity to pain. He entered our world of flesh and blood, tears and death. He suffered for us. Our sufferings become more manageable in the light of his. There is still a question mark against human suffering, but over it we boldly stamp another mark, the cross which symbolizes divine suffering.[25]

We worship no distant God, a God who is 'afar off', but a God who has drawn near:

> For whatever reason God chose to make man as he is – limited and suffering and subject to sorrows and death – He had the honesty and the courage to take His own medicine. Whatever game He is playing with His creation, He has kept His own rules and played fair. He has Himself gone through the whole of human experience, from the trivial irritations of family life and lack of money to the worst horrors, pain, humiliation, defeat, despair

---

25 John R. W. Stott, *The Cross of Christ* (Leicester: Inter-Varsity Press, 1986), pp. 335–336.

and death. He was born in poverty and died in disgrace and felt it was all worthwhile.[26]

What was worthwhile? The answer: bringing us into a restored relationship with God and preparing something new which is to come in the future and in which he invites us to share.

This brings us to the fourth implication: that the incarnation *ensures our eternal future*. We are not to think of the incarnation simply as a past event which we celebrate at Christmas; it is a present and future reality. God became man and will never cease to be man. The Son is for ever 'enfleshed' in glory, and this guarantees our bodily dwelling in glory too. Calvin describes this as a 'wonderful exchange':

> This is the wonderful exchange which, out of his measureless benevolence, he has made with us: that, by his descent to earth, he has prepared an ascent into heaven for us; that, by taking on our mortality, he has conferred his immortality upon us; that, accepting our weakness, he has strengthened us by his power; that, receiving our poverty unto himself, he has transferred his wealth to us; that, taking the weight of our iniquity upon himself that had sore oppressed us, he clothed us with his righteousness.[27]

Firstfruits

Many writers in the early church made much of the biblical idea of the 'firstfruits' in relation to the continuing incarnation

---

26 Dorothy L Sayers, *Creed or Chaos? And Other Essays in Popular Theology* (London: Methuen, 1947), pp. 1–2..

27 John Calvin, *Institutes of the Christian Religion*, 2 vols. (ed. John T. McNeill; trans. Ford Lewis Battles; Philadelphia: Westminster, 1960), 2:1362 [4.17.2].

of Christ and our future hope. In Deuteronomy 26:8–11 Moses describes the response the people of Israel were to make to God:

> 'And the LORD brought us out of Egypt with a mighty hand and an outstretched arm, with great deeds of terror, with signs and wonders. And he brought us into this place and gave us this land, a land flowing with milk and honey. And behold, now I bring the first of the fruit of the ground, which you, O LORD, have given me.' And you shall set it down before the LORD your God and worship before the LORD your God. And you shall rejoice in all the good that the LORD your God has given to you and to your house, you, and the Levite, and the sojourner who is among you.

The offering of the firstfruits was a joyous occasion under the Old Covenant, a visible reminder of what God had done in redeeming his people who now belonged to him. The apostle Paul develops this theme in relation to Christians and the future bodily resurrection:

> But in fact Christ has been raised from the dead, the firstfruits of those who have fallen asleep. For as by a man came death, by a man has come also the resurrection of the dead. For as in Adam all die, so also in Christ shall all be made alive. But each in his own order: Christ the firstfruits, then at his coming those who belong to Christ. (1 Cor. 15:20–23)

Also, the Holy Spirit in believers is part of the firstfruits won for us by Christ, a pledge or down payment of the full harvest yet to come (Rom. 8:23). It is our union with Christ by faith wrought by the Holy Spirit which ensures that what happened to him will happen to us, and that where he is, so there shall we be.

In a sermon on 1 Timothy, John Chrysostom links our union with Christ, the ascension and continuing incarnation to the firstfruits:

> I rule Angels, He says, and so do you, through Him who is the First-fruits (1 Cor. 15:23). I sit on a royal throne, and you are seated with Me in Him who is the First-fruits. As it is said, 'He hath raised us up together and made us sit together in heavenly places in Christ Jesus' (Eph. 2:6). Through Him who is the First-fruits, Cherubim and Seraphim adore you, with all the heavenly host, principalities and powers, thrones and dominions. Disparage not your body, to which such high honours appertain, that the unbodied Powers tremble at it. But what shall I say? It is not in this way only that I have shown my love to you, but by what I have suffered. For you I was spit upon, I was scourged. I emptied myself of glory, I left My father and came to you, who hate Me and turn from Me, and loathe to hear My Name. I pursued you, I ran after you, that I might overtake you. I united and joined Myself to you.[28]

Again we see how the incarnation and atonement are woven together in one seamless garment. Christ is the firstfruits;

---

28 John Chrysostom, Homily 15, *Homilies on the First Epistle of Paul to Timothy*, in Philip Schaff, *A Select Library of Nicene and Post-Nicene Fathers of the Christian Church*, Series 1, vol. 13 (New York: Christian Literature Co., 1886–1900).

believers are the full harvest being prepared to inherit together with Christ a new heaven and earth.

He came down to earth from heaven; he returned from earth to heaven

There is a fallen natural bent to exalt man at the expense of God. In the fifth century BC, Protagoras pronounced, 'Man is the measure of all things.' At the time of the Renaissance, Leon Battista Alberti declared, 'A man can do all things if he will.' In the nineteenth century this self-confidence blossomed into an all-out anti-God campaign typified by Algernon Swinburne's 'Hymn of Man': 'Glory to Man in the highest! for Man is the master of all things!' But there is a sense in which it *was* God's plan for man to be 'the master of all things' – not independently of God but acting on behalf of God. This we see in Psalm 8, for example, quoted by the writer to the Hebrews:

> What is mankind that you are mindful of them,
>   a son of man that you care for him?
> You made them a little lower than the angels;
>   you crowned them with glory and honour
>   and put everything under their feet.
> (Heb. 2:6–8 NIV)

This is taken by the author as being fulfilled in Jesus, the incarnate, atoning, risen and ascended One:

> In putting everything under them, God left nothing that is not subject to them. Yet at present we do not see

everything subject to them. But we do see Jesus, who was made lower than the angels for a little while, now crowned with glory and honour because he suffered death, so that by the grace of God he might taste death for everyone. (Heb. 2:8–9 NIV)

At the very centre of the universe there is now a man, a member and representative of the human race. As we enter the divine throne room with John (Rev. 5) we find a man who enacts God's plan of redemption and judgment upon the earth for he sake of his suffering people and God's honour (Rev. 6 – 11). This is the place where angels bow in endless worship and the redeemed are engaged in endless song. It is here we see the visible manifestation of the invisible God, a man robed in glorified humanity, whose name is Emmanuel, Jesus – God with us. Furthermore, the God who is with us is also the God who is for us (*Deus pro nobis*). All that we have been exploring brings us to the pastoral paean of praise of the apostle Paul at the end of Romans 8:

we are more than conquerors through him who loved us. For I am sure that neither death nor life, nor angels nor rulers, nor things present nor things to come, nor powers, nor height nor depth, nor anything else in all creation, will be able to separate us from the love of God in Christ Jesus our Lord.
(Rom. 8:37–39)

Questions for reflection and discussion

- How might you respond to the objection, 'No-one has ever seen God, therefore we can't know what he is like'?

- Why does belief in 'the God of the cross' help us understand and cope with the problem of pain?
- Why can we be certain that nothing will ever 'be able to separate us from the love of God in Jesus Christ'? How will this influence your attitude to the future?

Prayer

O God, whose blessed Son was manifested that he might destroy the works of the devil, and make us the sons of God, and heirs of eternal life: Grant us, we beseech thee, that, having this hope, we may purify ourselves, even as he is pure; that, when he shall appear again with power and great glory, we may be made like unto him in his eternal and glorious kingdom; where with thee, O Father, and thee, O Holy Spirit, he liveth and reigneth, ever one God, world without end. Amen.

(Book of Common Prayer, Collect for the Sixth Sunday after the Epiphany)

For further reading

General introduction

Lane, Tony, *Exploring Christian Doctrine* (London: SPCK, 2013), chapters 13 and 14.

Letham, Robert, *The Message of the Person of Christ*, The Bible Speaks Today (Nottingham: Inter-Varsity Press, 2013).

Lewis, Peter, *The Glory of Christ* (London: Hodder & Stoughton, 1992).

Macleod, Donald, *A Faith to Live By* (Fearn, Ross-shire: Mentor, 1998), chapters 8 and 9.

Reeves, Michael, *Christ Our Life* (Milton Keynes: Paternoster Press, 2014).

More detailed discussion

Crisp, Oliver, *Divinity and Humanity: The Incarnation Reconsidered* (Cambridge: Cambridge University Press, 2007).

——, *God Incarnate: Explorations in Christology* (Edinburgh: T&T Clark, 2009).

——, *The Word Enfleshed: Exploring the Person and Work of Christ* (Grand Rapids: Baker Academic, 2016).

Griffiths, Jonathan, 'Hebrews and the Trinity', in Brandon D. Crowe and Carl R. Trueman (eds.), *The Essential Trinity* (London: Apollos, 2016), pp. 122–138.

Macleod, Donald, *The Person of Christ*, Contours of Christian Theology (Leicester: Inter-Varsity Press, 1998).

Sanders, Fred, and Issler, Klaus (eds.), *Jesus in Trinitarian Perspective: An Introductory Christology* (Nashville: Broadman & Holman, 2007).

Treier, Daniel J., 'Incarnation', in Michael Allen and Scott R. Swain (eds.), *Christian Dogmatics: Reformed Theology for the Catholic Church* (Grand Rapids: Baker Academic Press, 2016), pp. 216–242.

Wells, David F., *The Person of Christ: A Biblical and Historical Analysis of the Incarnation* (Westchester: Crossway, 1984).

Wellum, Stephen J., *God the Son Incarnate* (Wheaton: Crossway, 2016).

Index of Scripture references

Index of Scripture references